5th Edition

APPLYING
THE STRATEGIC
PERSPECTIVE

CQ Press, an imprint of SAGE, is the leading publisher of books, periodicals, and electronic products on American government and international affairs. CQ Press consistently ranks among the top commercial publishers in terms of quality, as evidenced by the numerous awards its products have won over the years. CQ Press owes its existence to Nelson Poynter, former publisher of the *St. Petersburg Times*, and his wife Henrietta, with whom he founded Congressional Quarterly in 1945. Poynter established CQ with the mission of promoting democracy through education and in 1975 founded the Modern Media Institute, renamed The Poynter Institute for Media Studies after his death. The Poynter Institute *(www.poynter.org)* is a nonprofit organization dedicated to training journalists and media leaders.

In 2008, CQ Press was acquired by SAGE, a leading international publisher of journals, books, and electronic media for academic, educational, and professional markets. Since 1965, SAGE has helped inform and educate a global community of scholars, practitioners, researchers, and students spanning a wide range of subject areas, including business, humanities, social sciences, and science, technology, and medicine. A privately owned corporation, SAGE has offices in Los Angeles, London, New Delhi, and Singapore, in addition to the Washington DC office of CQ Press.

5th Edition

Anna Getmansky
Alejandro Quiroz Flores

APPLYING THE STRATEGIC PERSPECTIVE

Problems and Models

Los Angeles | London | New Delhi
Singapore | Washington DC

Los Angeles | London | New Delhi
Singapore | Washington DC

FOR INFORMATION:

CQ Press
An Imprint of SAGE Publications, Inc.
2455 Teller Road
Thousand Oaks, California 91320
E-mail: order@sagepub.com

SAGE Publications Ltd.
1 Oliver's Yard
55 City Road
London EC1Y 1SP
United Kingdom

SAGE Publications India Pvt. Ltd.
B 1/I 1 Mohan Cooperative Industrial Area
Mathura Road, New Delhi 110 044
India

SAGE Publications Asia-Pacific Pte. Ltd.
3 Church Street
#10-04 Samsung Hub
Singapore 049483

Acquisitions Editor: Elise Frasier
Editorial Assistant: Nancy Loh
Production Editor: Laura Barrett
Copy Editor: Amy Marks
Typesetter: C&M Digitals (P) Ltd.
Proofreader: Joyce Li
Cover Designer: Karine Hovsepian
Marketing Manager: Jonathan Mason
Permissions Editor: Jennifer Barron

Printed in the United States of America.

Library of Congress Cataloging-in-Publication Data

Getmansky, Anna.

Applying the strategic perspective : problems and models, workbook / Anna Getmansky Carnegie Mellon University, Alejandro Quiroz Flores University of Essex. — Fifth edition.

pages cm
Rev. ed. of: Applying the strategic perspective / Leanne C. Powner. 4th ed. c2010.

Includes bibliographical references and index.

ISBN 978-1-4522-2800-6 (pbk. : alk. paper)

1. Quiroz Flores, Alejandro, 1976- 2. International relations—Problems, exercises, etc. 3. International relations—Study and teaching. 4. International relations—Mathematical models. 5. Strategic planning—Problems, exercises, etc. 6. Strategic planning—Study and teaching. I. Bennett, D. Scott. Applying the strategic perspective. II. Title.

JZ1242.B45 2013
327.101—dc23   2012046833

12 13 14 15 16 10 9 8 7 6 5 4 3 2 1

CONTENTS

TABLES AND FIGURES

FIGURES

NOTE TO STUDENTS

As you may have already discovered, the fourth edition of Principles of International Politics is a unique international relations textbook. Like other introductory texts, it attempts to give you a wide-ranging view of the field and its impressive body of scholarship. Yet, unlike most textbooks, Principles challenges you to analyze real political problems in a rigorous fashion using mathematical tools. Although the text will take you step by step through these analytic tools, applying them effectively requires practice. Applying the Strategic Perspective will help you do just that. It offers additional explanations, examples, and exercises to help you employ important theoretical concepts and technical skills. You will not find instruction for every subsection of every chapter of Principles. Instead, the workbook offers advice, information, and help on the text's most important technical methods.

HOW TO USE THIS BOOK

This is a book that is meant to be used—written in, scribbled on, and eventually torn up. As you work, you will find that you will need colored pens or pencils or highlighters and a simple calculator such as the ones on most cell phones or computers to solve some of the problems in this workbook. After you have worked through and solved exercises, your instructor may ask you to submit certain pages as homework. The workbook's pages are perforated to make this easy. We have endeavored to leave the space necessary for you to work right in the workbook, but in some cases, you may need more space to solve a problem than is provided. Should this occur, do your work on a separate sheet, write the answer in the workbook, and attach the sheet to the assignment. In other cases, you may simply want to follow along through the workbook as you read corresponding sections of the main text.

In general, when you see mathematical work in the text, you should consider working through the math alongside the text, and/or consulting this workbook for additional explanation. Don't let the math worry you: Principles uses absolutely no math beyond what the SAT and ACT cover. Whereas most textbooks are designed to be read with a highlighter in hand, this one works best with a pencil and notebook paper for working through the examples on your own. It is important that you feel comfortable using the technical methods as they are introduced because you will be asked to apply them again in later sections of the book. The examples and exercises on these pages should help as you become familiar with the tools of Principles and allow you to gain a deeper understanding of the strategic perspective in international relations. Don't be shy, though. Be sure to ask your instructor to clarify any point you do not understand.

Exercise I-1. *Core Arguments*

This chapter makes four important arguments about international politics. For each argument, consider these corresponding questions.

Argument 1: International affairs are consequences of rational actions.

What does rationality mean? Give an example (real or hypothetical) of a rational action and an example (real or hypothetical) of an action that is not considered to be rational according to the definition presented in the chapter.

_____

_____

_____

_____

_____

Argument 2: International relations cannot be separated from domestic politics or from foreign policy.

What are some domestic political factors that might affect international political actions or choices? Give an example of one of these factors affecting the foreign policy of your country. What are some international political factors that might affect domestic political actions or choices? Again, give a brief example from your country.

_____

_____

_____

_____

Argument 3: Leaders take actions—both domestic and international—because they want to stay in power.

Give an example of a leader taking an international action that, in your view, contributed to his or her retaining power. Give an example of a leader taking an international (or domestic) action that contributed to his or her losing power. What else, besides retaining personal power, might motivate leaders to act in certain ways?

_____

_____

_____

_____

Argument 4: Relations between nations and between leaders are driven by reasoned decision making and strategic considerations.

Think about some actions your country's leader has taken recently in international politics.

a) What are some alternative actions the leader could have taken in these situations, but did not? In other words, what were the leader's choices or options?

_____

_____

_____

_____

b) How do the leader's choices reflect strategic considerations—that is, the anticipated reactions of domestic and international actors? Why do you believe some of the other options were *not* chosen?

_____

_____

_____

_____

_____

Exercise I-2. *Theories, Titles, and Assumptions*

The titles below are actual books and articles in international relations. Based on the title alone, indicate on the line whether you think the article or book has a Neorealist (NR), Liberal (L), or Constructivist (C) approach to international relations.

a) "Cooperation under Anarchy" _____

b) "Normative Power Europe" _____

c) "The False Promise of International Institutions" _____

d) "Anarchy Is What States Make of It" _____

e) *Ruling the World: Power Politics and the Rise of Supranational Institutions* _____

f) "Between Regimes and Realism—Transnational Agenda Setting: Soviet Compliance with CSCE Human Rights Norms" _____

g) "State Power and International Trade" _____

h) "Why Comply? Social Learning and European Identity Change" _____

Exercise I-3. *Leaders' Personal Goals, Domestic Political Constraints, and International Strategic Considerations*

For each of the international situations below, identify one way in which the leaders' personal goals, their domestic political constraints, and their strategic considerations with regard to the other nation could influence the outcome of the situation.

a) Two countries are negotiating a treaty to reduce trade barriers between themselves.

Leaders' personal goals: _____

Domestic political constraints: _____

Strategic considerations with regard to the other nation: _____

b) China, Russia, Japan, and the US negotiate with North Korea over its nuclear weapons and missile testing programs.

Leaders' personal goals: _____

Domestic political constraints: _____

Strategic considerations with regard to the other nation: _____

c) The UN is deciding whether to send an international force to Syria to end the civil war, restore order in that country, and rebuild its government and economy.

Leaders' personal goals: _____

Domestic political constraints: _____

Strategic considerations with regard to the other nation: _____

d) Israel and the Palestinians negotiate a possible peaceful settlement of their conflict.

Leaders' personal goals: _____

Domestic political constraints: _____

Strategic considerations with regard to the other nation: _____

CHAPTER 1

EVALUATING ARGUMENTS ABOUT INTERNATIONAL POLITICS

Exercise 1-1. *Developing a Theory*

a) Suppose you are writing a scientific article about the NBA draft. You are interested in developing a theory about which players are more likely to get drafted by an NBA team. In one paragraph, specify your assumption(s), apply basic logic, and generate a prediction (or predictions) about which features make players more likely to be drafted by an NBA team.

_____

_____

_____

_____

b) What is the dependent variable in your theory?

_____

c) What is (are) the independent variable(s) in your theory?

_____

d) How would you test your theory empirically? What evidence would falsify your theory? What evidence would support your theory?

_____

_____

_____

_____

Exercise 1-2. *Developing a Theory in International Relations—the Case of Economic Sanctions*

The US and other governments have been increasingly using economic sanctions to extract policy concessions from other states. For example, the US has recently announced economic sanctions against Syria following the violent civil war in that country. Similarly, the US has imposed sanctions on Iran and on North Korea to coerce them to halt their nuclear and missile programs, as well as on Burma and Zimbabwe due to the human rights abuses in these countries. Despite the increasing popularity of sanctions as a foreign policy tool, there is no consensus as to their effectiveness in extracting policy concessions from states and entities that they target. Proponents of sanctions suggest that they may work if they impose costs that are sufficiently high to make sustaining the controversial policy less attractive for the sanctions' targets. An example often cited in support of the argument that sanctions could work is the case of South Africa, where it has been argued that sanctions played a key role in the weakening of the apartheid regime. Conversely, those who argue that economic sanctions are ineffective suggest that they may backfire by making the target more determined not to yield to international pressure, and more resolute in maintaining the controversial policies. Examples of failed sanctions include those imposed against the regime of Saddam Hussein after the first Gulf War.

a) Suppose you were studying the role of economic sanctions in promoting compliance of foreign governments with international human rights standards. What is the dependent variable? What is the independent variable?

_____

_____

_____

b) Think about a theory that might explain the effectiveness of sanctions. Under what conditions are sanctions more likely to be effective? Think about events or situations that might make the target more sensitive to the costs of sanctions. Propose an assumption (or a set of assumptions), apply logic, and derive a prediction (or a set of predictions) about the conditions that could increase the effectiveness of the sanctions.

_____

_____

_____

_____

_____

_____

c) How would you test your theory empirically? Which cases would you include in your empirical analysis?

_____

_____

_____

_____

Exercise 1-3. *Constructing Hypotheses*

Theories are constructed to answer questions about relationships between variables and to improve our ability to predict future events. Consider the following concepts:

- Regime type
- Income per capita
- Election year
- Defense spending
- Interstate conflict
- War
- Economic growth
- Imprisonment of political opponents
- Cross-border air pollution
- Peaceful resolution of conflicts
- Refugees
- Openness to international trade
- Tariffs
- Rainfall
- Geographical distance
- Genocide

- Criminal responsibility
- Women's rights
- Human trafficking
- Major powers
- Alliances
- Marine protected areas
- Compliance
- International organizations
- Multilateral peacekeeping
- Peace
- Colonial past
- Natural resources
- Domestic political opposition
- Cultural exchange
- Foreign aid
- Democratization

a) Propose at least three research questions using the above list of concepts.

_____

_____

b) Construct at least three different hypotheses that provide potential answers to these questions.

_____

_____

_____

c) Propose a way of testing each hypothesis.

_____

_____

_____

d) What evidence would falsify each hypothesis?

_____

_____

_____

Exercise 1-4. *Selecting among Competing Theories*

One of the most important and policy-relevant questions in international relations is whether membership in international treaties constrains future behavior of states. For example, are non-nuclear states that are members of the Nuclear Nonproliferation Treaty (NPT) less likely to acquire nuclear weapons than they would be if they did not join the NPT? Similarly, are states that join international human rights treaties less likely to commit human rights abuses than they would be if they were not members in these treaties? Two influential theories of international relations offer alternative answers to this question. One is the neorealist theory, and the other is the liberal theory. You read about them in the introduction section of the textbook.

a) Briefly outline the neorealist and the liberal answers to this question. What does each theory predict with regard to the effect of a treaty membership on states' future behavior?

_____

_____

_____

_____

_____

b) What assumptions does each theory make? How do their predictions follow from their assumptions?

_____

_____

_____

c) How would you decide which theory is better able to explain the effect of international treaties on member states' behavior? Which standards for comparing theories would you apply?

_____

_____

_____

_____

_____
_____
_____
_____

Exercise 1-5.   *Falsifying a Theory*

After the end of the Cold War, many international relations scholars had hypothesized about the effect of this change on international conflicts. One influential scholar, Samuel Huntington, offered the following prediction:

"It is my hypothesis that the fundamental source of conflict in this new world will not be primarily ideological or primarily economic. The great divisions among humankind and the dominating source of conflict will be cultural. Nation states will remain the most powerful actors in world affairs, but the principal conflicts of global politics will occur between nations and groups of different civilizations. The clash of civilizations will dominate global politics. The fault lines between civilizations will be the battle lines of the future."[1]

a) Which factors, according to Huntington, could explain conflict in the post–Cold War period? Which factor does Huntington believe to be the best explanation among the possible explanations he alluded to in the preceding paragraph?

_____
_____
_____
_____

b) In Huntington's theory, what is the dependent variable, and what is the main independent variable?

_____
_____
_____
_____

c) Do you think Huntington's theory is falsifiable? If yes, what evidence, in principle, could falsify his theory? If not, explain why you consider his theory to be unfalsifiable.

_____
_____
_____
_____

d) How would you apply the first principle of wing walking to decide whether we should abandon the traditional explanations of conflict that focused on power in favor of Huntington's cultural explanation of conflict?

_____
_____
_____
_____

[1] Samuel P. Huntington, "The Clash of Civilizations?" *Foreign Affairs*, Summer 1993, p. 22.

Exercise 1-6.   *Necessary and Sufficient Conditions*

a) Suppose we wanted to test whether membership in the same international organizations makes countries more likely to cooperate. We collected the following data that describe the extent of correlation between membership in the same international organizations and an increase in cooperation. Based on table 1.1 below, determine whether membership in international organizations is a necessary, a sufficient, a necessary and sufficient, or neither a necessary nor a sufficient condition for an increase in cooperation. Explain your answer in one to two sentences.

TABLE 1.1

International Organization Membership and Cooperation

		Increase in Cooperation	
		Yes	No
Members in the Same International Organization	Yes	10	2
	No	1	20

_____

_____

_____

b) Suppose you wanted to test the prediction that the religious differences between neighboring states are sufficient to produce an interstate conflict. You collected 100 observations of dyads of neighboring states with and without conflict, and with and without religious differences. In table 1.2 below, propose a hypothetical distribution of observations that would be consistent with the argument that religious differences between two neighboring states are sufficient to ignite a conflict between them. What evidence would falsify this argument?

TABLE 1.2

Religious Differences and Conflict

		Conflict	
		Yes	No
Different Religion	Yes		
	No		

_____

_____

_____

c) Suppose you wanted to test the theory that democracy is a necessary condition for compliance with international human rights norms. You collected data on 200 countries, their regime type, and their human rights record in 2010. In table 1.3 below, indicate what a possible distribution of the observations would look like if this argument were correct. What evidence would falsify this argument?

TABLE 1.3

Democracy and Compliance with Human Rights Norms

Compliance with Human Right Norms

		Yes	No
Democracy	Yes		
	No		

_____

_____

_____

Exercise 1-7. *Selection Bias*

a) A prominent theory in international relations suggests that an arms race inevitably leads to a war. How would you test this theory empirically? Can you use a single case study to test it? What evidence would support this theory, and what evidence would falsify it?

_____

_____

_____

_____

b) How would you test the argument that ethnic divisions within a country increase the probability of a civil war? What universe of cases would you consider? What evidence would you expect to find if the argument is correct? What evidence could falsify this argument?

_____

_____

_____

_____

c) Suppose you read a study on the effect of membership in a regional organization (such as the European Union) on the convergence of states' preferences. For all state members of a certain regional organization, the study examines their positions on various issues in the year the regional organization is established and then 10 years after its establishment. Suppose the study finds a significant convergence in members' positions after 10 years of membership in that organization. Do you think this evidence supports the argument that membership in regional organizations leads to preference convergence among state members? Can you think of an alternative explanation for this finding? How would you empirically test the argument that membership in regional organizations leads to preference convergence?

_____

_____

_____

_____

CHAPTER 2

THE STRATEGIC PERSPECTIVE

Exercise 2-1. *Tyrantia and Democratia*

a) Fill in table 2.1 with the key characteristics of Tyrantia and Democratia.

Exercise 2-2. *Winning Coalitions and Private Goods*

For parts a, b, and c, write an expression or equation that says the same thing as the verbal statement. You will want to use some of the following symbols: $+$, $-$, $*$, $/$, $<$, $\leq$, $>$, and $\geq$. Please use the variable names indicated in parentheses.

a) The size of the winning coalition (W) can never exceed the size of the selectorate (S), but the two may be equal.

_____

_____

_____

TABLE 2.1

Key Characteristics of Tyrantia and Democratia

Characteristic	Tyrantia	Democratia
Population		
Selectorate		
Winning Coalition		
Revenue		
Per Capita Tax Take		

b) A government's revenues (R) are composed of foreign aid (f), natural resource wealth (n), and taxes levied at some rate t ($0 < t < 1$) on all production in the country (y).

_____

_____

_____

c) Consider a situation in which a leader answers to a small winning coalition (W). The leader has no need to provide public goods to his people, since his government rests entirely on a small band of cronies (i.e., the members of W). Write an equation to show the amount of private goods (z) that each person gets if the leader distributes all of the country's revenue equally among the winning coalition and himself. (*Hint:* The leader is not part of the winning coalition.)

_____

_____

_____

d) Consider your response to part c of this exercise. For simplicity, let's assume that $R = 10$. If a leader has one member in his W, what is the amount of private goods (z) that each person gets? Complete table 2.2 for different values of W and graph your values for $W = 1, 2, \ldots 10$ in figure 2.2. (Leave the column marked z' empty for now.)

e) Based on your graph, what is the effect on z of increasing the size of the winning coalition? Why?

_____

_____

_____

f) Consider a situation in which a foreign country makes a donation of foreign aid to the leader's state that is worth 2 units. Again, the leader has no interest in using this money to provide public goods and intends to distribute it as a private good. What is the new value of z—call it z'—for this larger pool of revenue? Complete the z' (say "z-prime") column in table 2.2 and add it to your graph in a different color. (Please provide a key for your instructor.)

TABLE 2.2

Winning Coalition Size and Private Goods

W	z	z′
1		
2		
3		
4		
5		
6		
7		
8		
9		
10		
100		

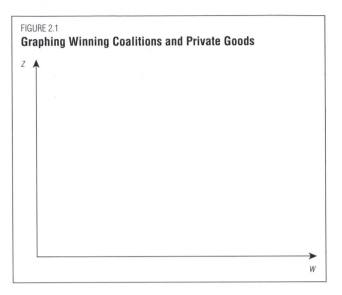

FIGURE 2.1
Graphing Winning Coalitions and Private Goods

Exercise 2-3. *Institutions and Preferences*

For the purposes of this exercise, let's normalize S to 1. You can interpret S, then, as 100 percent, and W as the percentage of people in S who are in W. (Think of a pie graph in which the whole circle is S [$S = 1$] and some shaded area represents W.)

a) Write an expression that shows the probability that a member of S is also a member of W.

_____

_____

_____

b) Write an expression that shows the probability that a member of S is *not* a member of W.

_____

_____

_____

c) If each member of W gets z in each period, how much benefit should a member of S expect to get in each period? (*Hint:* Review your responses to the previous parts of this question. How much does each member of W get, and how likely is she or he to get it?)

_____

_____

_____

Consider that a potential challenger exists, and you, as a member of W, are thinking about defecting from the current leader to support the challenger. As a current member of W, you get some amount of private goods z with certainty (i.e., with probability 1) in the current period and in every future period that you remain a member of W. But the challenger has offered you some new amount of private goods, z^*. If you defect and cause the current leader to fall, there is some chance (let's call it p) that you'll be a member of W in the next period, and you would get z^* from the challenger. There is also some chance, however, that you will *not* be in W—perhaps the challenger is unsuccessful or turns on you after entering office—and thus you might get 0 in the next period.

d) Write an expression that shows how much you'd expect to get in the next period if you stay with the current leader.

_____
_____
_____

e) Write an expression that shows how much you'd expect to get if you defect to the challenger in the next period. (*Hint:* What benefit do you get if you are in *W*, and how likely are you to get it? What benefit do you get if you are *not* in *W*, and how likely are you to get it?)

_____
_____
_____

f) How much does the challenger have to offer you to gain your support, relative to what you're getting from the current leader? Would you defect if $z = z^*$? If $z < z^*$? If $z > z^*$? (*Hint:* You want to take the action that maximizes your benefits. Manipulate your responses to the previous two items for this question.)

_____
_____
_____

Let's put the pieces together now.

g) If you are a member of *S* who is not currently in *W*, would you prefer *W* to be larger or smaller? Why? (*Hint:* Think about the pie graph.)

_____
_____
_____

h) If you are a member of *W*, would you support reforms to the government that increased the size of *W*? Why or why not?

_____
_____
_____

i) If you are a member of *W*, would you prefer that *S* be larger or smaller? Why?

_____
_____
_____

j) Think again about the probability that a member of *S* is in *W* in a future period. If you are the leader, and you believe you will be, at some point in your tenure you will face a challenger. If you want to make your position more secure, what kinds of institutional reforms (i.e., adjustments to the size of *W* or *S*) could you make? Why would these help you retain power?

_____
_____
_____
_____
_____

Exercise 2-4. *The Loyalty Norm*

Let's take a closer look at some of the expressions we wrote in the preceding exercise. If you are a member of the current winning coalition, then

$$p(z^*) + (1-p)(0) > z \qquad\qquad p = \frac{W}{S}$$

If this condition is met, you defect and support the challenger. Remember that z is the value of private goods you get from the leader right now, and z^* is some amount of private goods that a potential challenger has offered you if you defect from the current leader. The ratio of W to S, known as p, tells you how likely you are to be in a new leader's winning coalition, assuming that the size of the selectorate and the size of the winning coalition remain the same from the old leader to the new one.

a) Simplify the two expressions above by substituting the expression for p into the first equation and combining terms.

_____

_____

_____

b) Look at your new expression. Based on your intuition and your work in exercises 2-2 and 2-3, what do you think will happen to the left side of the equation as W/S gets smaller? What will have to happen to the value of z^* to make you still prefer the challenger to the current leader—will a low probability of being in the new winning coalition mean that the challenger has to offer you more or less private goods to gain your support?

_____

_____

_____

_____

c) Think about what your expression means. Would you always prefer to take the challenger's offer, z^*? After all, 6 is greater than 5. Why or why not?

_____

_____

_____

Graphing the Relationship

The next several questions ask you to evaluate your expression from part a of this exercise for different values of W and S and then to graph your results on figures 2.2 and 2.3. In both figures, assume that z, your private benefit now from the current leader, is equal to 5 units (i.e., $z = 5$). Call your benefit B.

d) Assume for now that $S = 10$ and that $z^* = 6$. For each value of W in table 2.3, evaluate your expression from part a and note it in the table. (The center column, W/S, is there for your computational convenience.) Graph your results in figure 2.2 and connect the points with a line.

e) Draw a line in figure 2.2 that represents your current benefits, that is, $z = B = 5$. You may wish to use a different color.

f) Continue to assume that $z^* = 6$. This time, we'll fix $W = 2$. For each value of S in table 2.4, evaluate your expression from part a and note it in the table. (The center column, W/S, is there for your computational convenience.) Graph your results in figure 2.3 and connect the points with a line.

TABLE 2.3

Evaluating Values of *w*

W	W/S	B
1		
2		
3		
4		
5		
6		
7		
8		
9		
10		

FIGURE 2.2

Graphing Values of *w*

B ▲

w/s

g) Draw a line in figure 2.3 that represents your current benefits, that is, $z = B = 5$. You may wish to use a different color.

h) Consider your graph in figure 2.2. How sure must you be that you'll be in the new winning coalition—what is the critical value of W/S—that makes you prefer the challenger's offer of $z^* = 6$ over the current leader's $z = 5$? (*Hint:* Think about the two lines you graphed.) Is this a high value of p, or a relatively low one?

i) Consider your graph in figure 2.3. How sure must you be that you'll be in the new winning coalition—what is the critical value of W/S—that makes you prefer the challenger's offer of $z^* = 6$ over the current leader's $z = 5$? Is this a high value of p, or a relatively low one?

j) Think about your responses to the previous two questions. Are you willing to join the challenger at very low levels of p? Why do you think this is true? (*Hint:* Think about the values of z and z^*.)

k) Imagine that p is very low—say, 0.1. Under these conditions, how much does the challenger have to offer you—what is the critical value of z^*—to gain your support? (*Hint:* Remember that you are currently getting $z = 5$ from the leader.)

Exercise 2-5. *More on Loyalty*

Figure 2.4 in *Principles* presents the estimated sizes of the winning coalition and the selectorate for 10 countries in 2006.

TABLE 2.4

Evaluating Values of S

S	W/S	B
1		
2		
3		
4		
5		
6		
7		
8		
9		
10		

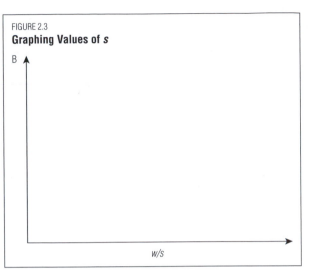

FIGURE 2.3

Graphing Values of s

a) Based on the information provided in figure 2.4 in *Principles*, discuss the probability of defection in China relative to Russia.

_____

_____

_____

b) Now discuss the probability of defection in Syria relative to Russia.

_____

_____

_____

c) In which countries do you expect to see more leadership turnover? Why?

_____

_____

_____

Exercise 2-6.

List the selectorate theory's five rules of governance and explain the logic behind them.

_____

_____

_____

CHAPTER 3

TOOLS FOR ANALYZING INTERNATIONAL AFFAIRS

THE MEDIAN VOTER THEOREM

The median voter theorem is a powerful tool to analyze social choice. The simple argument of this theorem is that in a group of voters arrayed along some continuous policy dimension, the median voter holds the critical position that will determine the outcome of decisions. That is, the position of the median voter will be the winning position.

Three critical conditions must hold before we can use the median voter theorem to predict outcomes. Actors must have (or be assumed to have) single-peaked preferences, we must have a *unidimensional issue area*, and decisions must be made by a majority rule.

Exercise 3-1. *The Power of the Median Voter*

a) Why is the median voter in such a powerful position? Explain, either intuitively or using one or more numerical examples to demonstrate.

_____

_____

_____

_____

b) Under what conditions does the median voter theorem apply? In which cases can we not use the median voter theorem to predict the winning position?

_____

_____

_____

Exercise 3-2. *Unidimensionality*

a) Provide an example of a unidimensional policy issue related to international relations. You can use recent topics mentioned in the news, or historical examples. What makes this policy unidimensional? What would make it not unidimensional? Display the issue graphically.

_____

_____

b) Using the example from part a, provide examples of three players who have different positions with regard to this issue, and locate their ideal points in the unidimensional policy space above.

_____

_____

Single-Peaked Preferences

The median voter theorem assumes single-peaked preferences in spatial models. Briefly, an actor with *single-peaked preferences* has one most preferred outcome on a given issue or dimension, and outcomes other than the ideal point give decreasing utility (are less valuable to the actor) as each outcome becomes more distant from the ideal point.

As a practical example, most of us have single-peaked preferences over the amount of sugar in our coffee (or tea). Suzy has an ideal point of three spoonfuls of sugar in a cup of coffee. This point makes her happiest. If she has single-peaked preferences and an ideal point of three spoonfuls, then no amount of sugar gives her greater utility than three spoonfuls. Her utility function (a line or curve showing how an actor's utility changes over different values of variables) peaks at three and, with an assumption of single-peaked preferences, decreases on either side of three without rising again. If for whatever reason Suzy couldn't have 3 spoonfuls of sugar, she would be equally happy with 2.5 spoonfuls *or* with 3.5 spoonfuls, since these are equally distant from her ideal point. As a general rule, actors with single-peaked preferences prefer points closer to their ideal point to those farther away from it, so 2.5 spoons is preferred to 5 spoons, since 2.5 is nearer to the ideal point than 5 is. (Examine figure 3.1 to verify that these relationships hold and to familiarize yourself with how this works.)

In contrast, non-single-peaked preferences have a utility function that reaches a peak at the ideal point and declines, but then turns back upward. This implies that the actor's utility does not continue to decline as he or she moves away from the ideal point—on the contrary, at that bottom point the utility starts to increase again, even though the distance from the ideal point is increasing. If Suzy can't have 3 spoonfuls, she'd next prefer 2 or 4 spoonfuls, but if she couldn't have 2 or 4 she'd rather have 6 spoonfuls. This just doesn't make sense.

Exercise 3-3. *Single-Peaked Preferences*

a) Draw the non-single-peaked utility function described on figure 3.1. (*Hint:* Think about what "to like something more" means in terms of the axes of figure 3.1.)

b) Explain in one sentence what single-peaked preferences mean.

_____

_____

_____

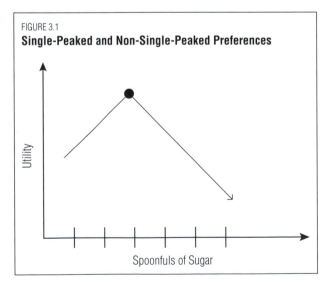

FIGURE 3.1
Single-Peaked and Non-Single-Peaked Preferences

Utility

Spoonfuls of Sugar

c) Also on figure 3.1, draw the utility function for an actor whose ideal point is 0 (zero) spoons of sugar. (Please use a dashed line or a different color.) Is this utility function single-peaked? Defend your answer.

_____

_____

_____

Exercise 3-4. *Majority Rule*

Consider three states (Alphaland, Betaland, and Gammaland) that have to choose among three levels of greenhouse gas emissions (Low, Medium, and High). The states' preferences are shown in table 3.1.

a) If decisions are made using a majority rule, which green-house gas emission level is going to prevail against any other alternative? Explain why.

Now consider the following preferences over outcomes in table 3.2:

a) What changed compared to table 3.1?

b) How does the change identified in part b affect the outcome? Continue to assume that decisions are made using a majority rule. Which greenhouse gas emission level is going to prevail against any other alternative based on table 3.2?

TABLE 3.1

Preferences of Three Hypothetical States over Greenhouse Emissions

Preference	Alphaland	Betaland	Gammaland
First	High	Low	Medium
Second	Medium	Medium	Low
Third	Low	High	High

TABLE 3.2

Preferences of Three Hypothetical States over Greenhouse Emissions for Exercise 3-4b

Preference	Alphaland	Betaland	Gammaland
First	High	Low	Medium
Second	Medium	High	Low
Third	Low	Medium	High

c) In light of the previous discussion of single-peaked preferences, which state does not have such preferences, according to table 3.2?

The Median Voter Theorem in International Affairs

Exercise 3-5. *The North American Free Trade Agreement*
It's early 1992, and the United States (USA), Mexico (MEX), and Canada (CAN) are wrapping up negotiations on the North American Free Trade Agreement (NAFTA).

Environmental Standards I

Environmental regulation is costly to business, and it may undercut Mexico's comparative advantage in cheap labor. Canadians, on the other hand, care strongly about the environment. Under Republican president George H. W. Bush (Bush senior), the US is less concerned about environmental protection than under some previous administrations.

a) Consider the scenario modeled in figure 3.2. Using the median voter theorem, what is the outcome of this international negotiating situation? Which actor's ideal point is selected? Why?

FIGURE 3.2
Preferred Level of Environmental Protection Regulations I

Low   High

MEX   USA   CAN

Environmental Standards II

It's now early 1993. The November 1992 US presidential elections produced a rather unexpected upset of a sitting president, bringing Democrat Bill Clinton to the Oval Office with the support of a left-wing coalition of environmentalists, labor, and feminists.

b) What happens to the US position on labor standards as a result of this change in leadership?

_____

_____

c) Consider figure 3.3. According to the median voter theorem, which actor's ideal point is selected? What happens to the outcome of this situation, compared to the model in figure 3.2?

_____

_____

_____

FIGURE 3.3
Preferred Level of Environmental Protection Regulations II

Low   High

MEX   USA   CAN

Labor Standards

A number of US actors, especially US labor unions, were very concerned about the low level of labor standards (and particularly the very low wages) in Mexico. They feared that this cheap labor pool would cause many jobs to drain from the US to Mexico—a "giant sucking sound," as third-party conservative candidate Ross Perot described it. After Clinton is elected with the support of many traditional Democratic constituencies, including labor unions, adding labor standards to NAFTA becomes a significant objective.

d) Consider figure 3.4. According to the median voter theorem, what level of labor standards will be agreed on by the parties? How reasonable does this sound given what we know of the interests of the parties?

_____

_____

_____

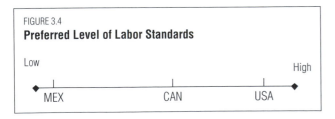

FIGURE 3.4
Preferred Level of Labor Standards

Low   High

MEX   CAN   USA

Weighting the Votes

Let's think about this situation again. All the actors in this situation may be individual sovereign states, but they are not equally powerful. Instead, let's assume that states' votes are weighted by their power. In other words, more powerful actors have more "votes" to cast on a given issue. Look at figures 3.2 and 3.3 again, but this time allocate 5 votes to Mexico, 10 votes to Canada, and 16 votes to the United States.

e) What is the median vote under these voting weights (how many votes are needed to win)? _____

f) In figure 3.3, who holds the median (weighted) vote? Is this actor the median voter? What happens to the outcome from part c of this exercise?

_____

_____

_____

g) Using the same distribution of votes, look at figure 3.4 again. Who holds the median (weighted) vote? Is this actor the median voter? What happens to the outcome from part d of this exercise?

_____

_____

_____

_____

h) What does this result suggest about why powerful countries usually get their way in bilateral or even multilateral international negotiations?

_____

_____

_____

i) *Challenge*: Devise a realistic distribution of votes in which the weighted voting outcome—the ideal point of the holder of the median vote—is the same as the ideal point of the median voter.

Exercise 3-6. *Preferences at Munich*

The median voter model in figure 3.5 depicts the situation at the Munich conference of 1938, when British prime minister Neville Chamberlain and his French and Italian counterparts had to decide what percentage of Hitler's demands for Czechoslovak territory to grant. The actors are Hungary (Hu), the United Kingdom (UK), France (F), Italy (I), Germany (G), Czechoslovakia (Cz), Belgium (B), Austria (A), and Poland (Po).

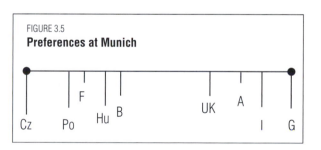

FIGURE 3.5
Preferences at Munich

a) If all actors in the model have one vote, who is the median voter? Is this actor's ideal point a plausible outcome for this situation? Why or why not?

_____

_____

_____

b) If "voting" in this situation is weighted by power, so that more powerful actors have more influence on the outcome, in which direction is the median vote likely to shift? Why?

_____

_____

c) The following voting weights for the actors in the model were developed using the Correlates of War Project's Composite Index of National Capabilities, representing each state's share of capabilities among these actors in

1938. Assuming these weights, which total 100 "votes," where would the outcome be? Is this more plausible than the answer to part b of this exercise? Why or why not?

Cz = 4	Hu = 2	A = 2
Po = 7	B = 3	I = 10
F = 13	UK = 21	G = 38

_____

_____

_____

_____

d) If possible, use your library's resources to obtain and read the cover story of the *New York Times* or the *Washington Post* from September 30, 1938. (If that's not possible, do a bit of research into Hitler's demands and the outcome of the Munich conference.) About where on the issue dimension did the true outcome fall? Does this agree with your model?

_____

_____

_____

_____

SPATIAL MODELING

Spatial modeling is a tool used to analyze behavior when actors have single-peaked preferences over two (or more) linked issues. (More than two issues is possible but more complicated; ask your instructor if you're curious.) Constructing a spatial model requires several pieces of information:

Information about the issues includes

- the choices, or options, arrayed on a separate scale for each issue, and
- the location of the *status quo*, or current outcome, for each issue.

Information about the actors includes

- the *ideal point*, or most preferred outcome, for each relevant actor on each issue, and
- the nature of each possible *winning coalition*, a set of actors who are able to change the status quo if they agree on a new solution.

As in the median voter theorem, we assume that preferences are single-peaked and that we can conceptualize the issues as single dimensions on which we can rank policy options.

Circular Indifference Curves

Chapter 3 introduced circular indifference curves. An *indifference curve* shows all the points with equal utility to the actor, that is, all the points among which the actor is indifferent. As we discussed earlier, in a spatial model (or any model assuming single-peaked preferences), increasing distance from the ideal point reflects decreases in utility. When actors have single-peaked preferences over two issues (and assuming that the actor cares equally about both issues), we find the set of points that have equal utility to the actor at an equal distance from the actor's ideal point. In two dimensions, this means that the indifference curves are circular, since all the points on a circle are equidistant from its center.

If we assume that the center point represents an actor's ideal point, then that actor will be indifferent to points above, below, or to the side of that preferred position, as long as those alternatives are equidistant from the ideal point. Points on the inside of any indifference curve are more preferred to points outside the curve because they are closer to the ideal point, and points outside the curve are less preferred than points on (or inside) the curve.

Circular indifference curves that pass through the status quo have a special property that makes them particularly useful for our purposes. When a curve is centered on an actor's ideal point and passes through the status quo, the curve describes the set of points that are of equal utility to the actor as the status quo. The assumption of single-peaked preferences implies that any point inside this curve is *better* for the actor than the status quo is, and so the actor would prefer that point to the status quo. Since we are looking for points that actors would accept over the status quo, this useful property of indifference curves that are tangent to the status quo makes these curves the only ones we usually draw.

If we draw these curves for several actors and find that the curves overlap, the actors whose curves overlap prefer any points inside that overlap area to the status quo or to any other points outside the curves. A *win set* is an area where these special indifference curves overlap for a *winning coalition*, a group of actors who are sufficiently influential on the issues to be able to change the status quo.

Constructing a Spatial Model

When we construct a spatial model, we make two important assumptions: The actors have single-peaked preferences, and the issues are arranged so that their options represent increasing levels on some scale. For example, in figure 3.6 in *Principles*, the issues are laid out so that moving right indicates an increasingly militarized nuclear policy and moving upward indicates a foreign response that uses rewards more than punishment. To construct a spatial model:

1. Identify the two linked issues. Draw a *separate* horizontal axis for each, taking care to describe the axes in terms of some increasing value. Each axis represents a unidimensional issue space, a graphical representation of a single issue.
2. Identify the actors' ideal points and the status quo for each issue, and locate these points on your issue axes.
3. Link your issues by turning one vertical, carefully matching the low ends of the individual axes. (The easiest way to do this is to trace one through a sheet of paper and then rotate the paper and trace or copy it into the new location.) Then, locate each actor's ideal point and the status quo in your new multidimensional issue space by following each from its point on the axis out into the center.
4. Construct circular indifference curves for each actor, where the curve centers on the actor's ideal point and is tangent to (passes through) the status quo.
5. Examine your model to locate any areas of overlap, and determine if those areas are win sets.

Exercise 3-7. *NAFTA II*

Exercise 3-5 asked you to consider the various issue areas of the NAFTA agreement separately. Now we consider them jointly in a single spatial model.

a) Figure 3.6 summarizes the information on actor preferences for environmental and labor standards in the NAFTA agreement. Transfer the ideal points and status quo from figure 3.6 onto figure 3.7 and locate these points in the new multidimensional space you've created. (*Hint:* Be sure to match the "low" ends of each scale at the origin.)

b) Because no prior agreement exists on these issues, the status quo is at the "low" endpoint of each axis. Draw circular indifference curves for each actor. Center the curve on the actor's ideal point, and make the radius equal to the distance from the ideal point to the status quo. (*Hint:* You may wish to use a different color for each actor to help you interpret the model.)

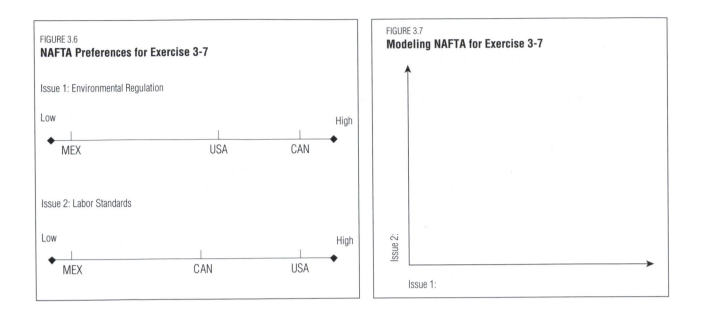

FIGURE 3.6
NAFTA Preferences for Exercise 3-7

Issue 1: Environmental Regulation

Low   High

MEX   USA   CAN

Issue 2: Labor Standards

Low   High

MEX   CAN   USA

FIGURE 3.7
Modeling NAFTA for Exercise 3-7

Issue 2:

Issue 1:

c) Assume unweighted voting and majority rule. Under these rules, what win sets exist in your model? Shade or otherwise indicate the win sets in your model. Which win set is most likely to contain the outcome, and why?

_____

_____

_____

d) Consider all the possible two-actor win sets that you found in part c of this exercise. Who is the median voter on each axis? (Assume unweighted voting.) Is this actor the same across both issue dimensions? Is the median actor(s) part of all the possible winning coalitions, or can the other two parties reach an agreement without the median actor's participation? Describe the win sets that do not involve the median actor(s) below, and indicate them on the figure with an asterisk.

_____

_____

_____

_____

e) Assume now that unanimous voting rules apply. Are there any win sets that satisfy all three actors? Discuss why or why not.

_____

_____

_____

Exercise 3-8. *The Doha Development Round*

The Doha Development Round of World Trade Organization (WTO) talks began in Doha, Qatar, in November 2001. Since then, negotiations have bogged down over two related issues: the level of protectionism in the developing world and the level of agricultural subsidies in the developed world. Less-developed countries prefer high levels of protection, particularly on manufactured products and technology, to protect their domestic producers who cannot compete effectively with the highly efficient producers of the developed world. On the other hand, firms in developed countries benefit from lower protection since this enhances their export prospects. Of course, some variation exists among both of these groups, based on characteristics of the economy.

Agricultural protection is a politically salient issue in many developed countries. This is particularly true in the European Union, in which agricultural subsidies consume an enormous (although shrinking) portion of the budget, and in the US. Government agricultural subsidies enable producers to sell at a lower price than the cost of production, so products are cheaper and more competitive with goods produced in countries with lower costs of production. The ideal points of a select set of WTO members are shown in figure 3.8. Use this information to construct a spatial model in figure 3.9.

a) Transfer the ideal points and status quo from figure 3.8 onto figure 3.9 and locate these points in the new multidimensional space you've created. (*Hint:* Be sure to match the "low" ends of each scale at the origin.)

b) Draw circular indifference curves for each actor. Center the curve on the actor's ideal point, and make the radius equal to the distance from the ideal point to the status quo. (*Hint:* You may wish to use a different color for each actor to help you interpret the model.)

c) Several winning coalitions are possible. The US and EU must be included in any winning coalition. Possible winning coalitions include: US, EU, Canada, and China; and US, EU, Canada, India, and Mexico. Identify the win sets, if any, that correspond to these winning coalitions. Shade them in some color on your model (please include a key). Which of these win sets is most likely to contain the outcome? Why?

_____

_____

_____

d) Based on your model, in which direction is policy most likely to move? Compare the relative positions of the status quo and the most probable outcome(s) on each dimension.

_____

_____

_____

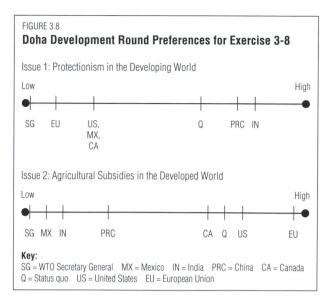

FIGURE 3.8
Doha Development Round Preferences for Exercise 3-8

Issue 1: Protectionism in the Developing World

Key:
SG = WTO Secretary General   MX = Mexico   IN = India   PRC = China   CA = Canada
Q = Status quo   US = United States   EU = European Union

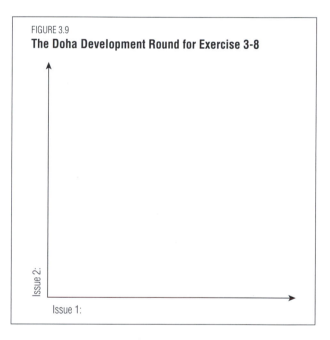

FIGURE 3.9
The Doha Development Round for Exercise 3-8

_____

_____

e) What, if any, potential outcomes from these negotiations are acceptable to the WTO secretary general? What role can the WTO secretary general play in these negotiations, and why might he have an incentive to do this?

_____

_____

_____

_____

_____

f) Use the WTO website (http://www.wto.org) or news sources to find the current status of this dispute. If the dispute has been resolved, does the resolution seem to match your prediction? If the dispute has not been resolved, what is the continued cause of delay?

_____

_____

_____

_____

_____

Exercise 3-9. *Domestic Politics and Spatial Modeling: China and Taiwan*

The biggest potential flashpoint in East Asian security is the ongoing dispute between the Republic of China on Taiwan (*T*) and the People's Republic of China (Mainland China, *M*), over their reintegration into a single country under Beijing's control. Simplifying slightly, Taiwanese preferences have historically been to preserve

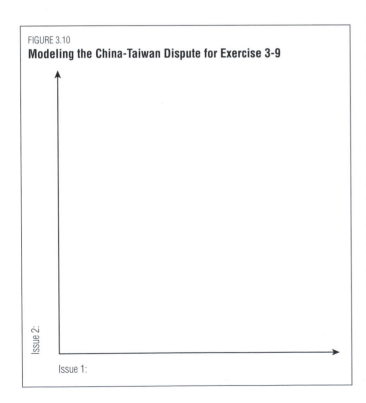

FIGURE 3.10
Modeling the China-Taiwan Dispute for Exercise 3-9

Issue 2:

Issue 1:

much autonomy (low integration), while at the same time preserving a high level of peace and security in the region. The status quo is only slightly different from Taiwan's preferred outcome; security is a bit lower and the countries are a bit too integrated for the Taiwanese government's taste.

Mainland China's position is much harder to determine. In the absence of a free press, little reliable information on the Chinese Communist Party's (CCP) internal politics escapes. Taiwanese leaders believe that one of three (hypothetically) possible groups of CCP leaders actually dominates policymaking. The first, M_1, is concerned about the party's internal status in the face of a shaky domestic economy and believes that diverting attention to the Taiwan issue could help preserve order at home. This group prefers a high level of integration, even at the cost of very low security in the region, and is willing to make substantial threats toward Taiwan. It may or may not be willing to actually *use* military force, but it is at least willing to threaten regional security.

M_2, by contrast, is the result of a power struggle within the CCP: a faction closely tied to the People's Liberation Army (PLA) and a faction interested in gaining capitalist-style investment for the ailing economy have allied to influence policy. This group is willing to invade Taiwan, if necessary, to achieve complete reintegration of the societies (and more important, their economies). It prefers high economic integration and a fairly low level of security.

Finally, the politicians of M_3 are entirely concerned with the state of the domestic economy and believe that the party's hegemony may be threatened if it does not make efforts *soon* to reduce unemployment and increase capital stock. To this group, international military adventures would destabilize the society and the economy and should be avoided at all costs; they are hopeful that Taiwan will react positively and relax some of its restrictions on doing business with the mainland. They would prefer higher regional security and also higher levels of economic integration than currently exist.

a) Construct a spatial model in figure 3.10 showing the issues in contention, Taiwan, the status quo, and the three possible types of mainland China. Indicate any win sets that may exist. (You may wish to use different colors to clarify your model; if you do, please provide a key.)

b) Is an agreement to change the status quo possible? (*Hint:* What actors constitute a winning coalition here?) With which type(s) of mainland China could Taiwan make an agreement, and which way would the status quo move?

_____

_____

c) Assume that the mainland economy goes into a recession, and party control is threatened. After a major internal leadership struggle and some violence, the faction allied with the PLA (M_2) takes charge. Taiwanese leaders fear that the status quo is unacceptable to these new leaders—that it produces less benefit for them (is too far from their ideal point) than other potential outcomes, which the new mainland leadership might try to take by force. While using force to take Taiwan would be costly, the mainland leaders might consider it if they expected large benefits that would substantially exceed the costs. This implies that the mainland's reservation point, its smallest acceptable negotiated outcome, is equal to its costs of taking Taiwan by force. If the mainland leadership's reservation point is closer to the leadership's ideal point than the status quo currently is, is agreement possible? Draw a new indifference curve for M_2 on your model (please use another color) to reflect the new government's reservation point. In most of our other spatial models, what was the outcome if no win set existed? What is the likely outcome here?

_____

_____

_____

_____

d) Taiwan is approaching presidential elections, and the current president's party is unable to field a credible candidate. The first contender, from party A, has categorically refused all integration, even in the face of severe pressure from the mainland; he has vowed to defend the country but will not strike preemptively. Party B's contender, on the other hand, promotes relaxing restrictions on economic interaction with the mainland in an effort to preserve regional peace and security. Add A's and B's ideal points to your model. (If your model is already full, please trace it onto another sheet of paper and then do this stage.) Assuming that the status quo represents the minimum acceptable utility for either candidate, is a peaceful settlement possible now between either contender and the mainland? If so, with whom, and in what direction will the status quo shift?

_____

_____

_____

EXPECTED UTILITY

Recall that expected utility is created simply by multiplying the utility of outcomes by the probability that they will actually happen, summing the results over the set of possible outcomes. So, if there are two possible outcomes to a choice, we could write the following:

$$EU_{choice} = (probability_{outcome\ 1})\ (U_{outcome\ 1}) + (probability_{outcome\ 2})\ (U_{outcome\ 2})$$

More generally,

$$EU_{choice} = (probability_1)\ (U_{outcome\ 1}) + (probability_2)\ (U_{outcome\ 2}) + \ldots + (probability_x)\ (U_{outcome\ x}),$$

where x is the number of possible outcomes.

Exercise 3-10. *Buying a Lottery Ticket I*
   A lottery ticket has a lot of utility if you win. But the odds of winning are small, and if you lose, you get nothing. In the first ticket in table 3.3, the expected utility of the ticket is $0.10. Calculate the expected utility of the second lottery ticket in table 3.3.

Exercise 3-11. *Starting a War*

Consider what happens if you start a war with another country. Calculate the expected utility in the situations in table 3.4.

TABLE 3.3
Expected Utility of Two Lottery Tickets for Exercise 3-10

p_{win}	U_{Win}	p_{lose}	U_{lose}	$EU = p_{win}(U_{win}) + p_{lose}(U_{lose})$
.00001	$10,000	0.99999	0	0.00001($10,000) + 0.99999($0) = $0.10
.001	$2,500	0.999	0	

TABLE 3.4
Expected Utility of Different War Situations for Exercise 3-11

	p_{win}	U_{Win}	p_{lose}	U_{lose}	$EU_{war} = p_{win}(U_{win}) + p_{lose}(U_{lose})$
A	0.60	5,000	0.40	−5,000	0.60(5,000) + 0.40(−5,000) = 1,000
B	0.75	5,000	0.25	−5,000	3750 + -1250 37500 .75(5000)+ .25(-5000)=2500
C	0.45	5,000	0.55	−5,000	.45(5000) + .55(-5000) = 2250 - 2750 = -500
D	0.60	10,000	0.40	−2,000	.6(10000) + .4(-2000) = 6000 - 800 = 5200

Decision Theory

Decision theory is the decision-making model that tells us that given a set of options, or choices, and given an *expected utility* of each option, decision makers will choose the option with the greatest expected utility.

We typically write the condition that given two options, A and B, if $EU_A > EU_B$, the decision maker will choose A. If $EU_A < EU_B$, the decision maker will choose B. If the expected utilities are equal, the decision maker does not care—that is, he or she is indifferent between the two options.

Consider the expected value of the lottery tickets listed in table 3.3. Based on your odds of winning and the payout, the first ticket had an expected value of ten cents. Let us suppose the ticket cost $1.00. So if you don't buy the ticket you keep $1.00, meaning that the expected value of not buying the ticket is $1.00.

According to decision theory, is it rational to buy the ticket if your utility for money is equal to the quantity of money? The answer is no. Why not? Because $EU_{buy} = \$0.10$, while $EU_{don't\ buy} = \$1.00$.

To review how to calculate expected utility, see the Walk-Through on the website: http://bdm.cqpress.com.

Exercise 3-12.   *Buying a Lottery Ticket II*
Based on your odds of winning, the second ticket in table 3.3 had an expected value of $2.50 (if you calculated correctly). The ticket costs $1.00. Is it rational to buy the ticket? Why or why not?

_____

_____

Exercise 3-13.   *The Choice of Where to Go to College*
Before going to college, you made an expected utility calculation about where to send your application, and then once you were admitted, where to choose to attend.

Assume you are deciding to apply to one of three universities: Harvard University, Pennsylvania State University, and East Appalachian State University.

- The utility, or net benefit, of going to Harvard would be great. You would graduate and expect to get a high-paying job, perhaps worth $80,000 or more annually. However, knowing your school record, you might assess the probability that you would 1) be admitted, and 2) graduate with a decent record, to be fairly low—only 30 percent. This implies there is a 70 percent chance you will not complete the degree and be unemployed.
- The utility of going to Penn State is good. Graduates make a good ($40,000) salary on average, and you think it is likely (75 percent) that you will be admitted and will graduate with a good record.
- The utility of East Appalachian State is, unfortunately, not so great. Graduates earn only $20,000 on average. Its advantage is that you are very certain (95 percent) that you will be admitted and will graduate successfully.
- Assume the utility of not going to college, or of going to college and not completing the degree successfully, is 0.

These values are represented in table 3.5.

a) Compute the expected utility of each option in table 3.5 and write it in the table.

TABLE 3.5
Expected Utility of Different Universities for Exercise 3-13

College	Utility (rough, ordinal)	Probability of Admission and Graduation (rough, ordinal)	Utility (precise, cardinal)	Prob. (precise)	Expected Utility
Harvard	Excellent	Low	80,000	30%	
Penn State	Good	Good	40,000	75%	
E. Appalachian State	Low	Excellent	20,000	95%	

b) Which college is the best rational choice in this situation? Why?

_____

_____

Solving for Critical Conditions

Sometimes we want to solve expected utility equations for certain *critical conditions*. By doing this, we find the value of p that is a "tipping point"—the probability of success that makes selecting one choice better than another. Two important steps are involved in solving for critical conditions:

1. Take the various choices (usually two) that the decision maker might select, and set the expected utility of the two equations (choices) equal to each other. (Even if you are given probabilities, don't use them; substitute the variable p instead.)

2. Solve algebraically for the condition of interest (usually p). The solution gives the value of the condition at which the decision maker is *indifferent* between the two choices. Given that we know where he or she is indifferent, if the value of the condition changes just a little bit, it will be enough to tip the decision maker one way or the other.

In exercise 3-13, Penn State was the rational choice of where to attend college. An important question we can answer is, at what point is attempting to attend Harvard rational? That is, what is the critical condition at which $EU_{Harvard}$ becomes greater than $EU_{Penn\ State}$?
To determine this:

- Set the two choices (Harvard and Penn State) equal to each other.

$$EU_{Harvard} = EU_{Penn\ State}$$
$$(p_{get\ into\ Harvard})(U_{Harvard}) = (p_{get\ into\ Penn\ State})(U_{Penn\ State})$$

- Solve algebraically for the condition of interest. In this case we are interested in learning the critical value of $p_{get\ into\ Harvard}$—that is, how sure we must be that we will successfully graduate (what value p must have)—before we should apply to Harvard. Only one step needs to be done in the algebra, dividing both sides by $U_{Harvard}$.

$$p_{get\ into\ Harvard} = (p_{get\ into\ Penn\ State})(U_{Penn\ State})/U_{Harvard}$$

We could now find this value of p numerically. Recall that $U_{Harvard} = 80,000$, $p_{get\ into\ Penn\ State} = 0.75$, and $U_{Penn\ State} = 40,000$. (Since we are solving for $p_{get\ into\ Harvard}$, we do not insert that value from the prior table.) So:

$$p_{get\ into\ Harvard} = (0.75)(40,000)/80,000 = 0.375$$

This critical probability of 0.375 indicates that if you believe your chances of getting into Harvard and graduating are more than 37.5 percent, then applying to Harvard would be better than applying to Penn State.

Exercise 3-14. *Military Attack*

War is an expensive proposition. When considering a military attack, leaders are always uncertain who will win, although they are usually somewhat more certain about what the future holds if they remain at peace. This leads to the following typical situation of deciding what to do in war:

U_{peace} is certain; it is the value of peace, or of the status quo. This is sometimes designated U_{SQ}, or $U_{don't\,attack}$. EU_{war} is based on risks, so a leader is uncertain how war will turn out because his state might win or might lose. The equation for the expected utility is

$$EU_{war} = (p_{win})\,(U_{win}) + (p_{lose})\,(U_{lose}).$$

a) How does the equation $EU_{war} = (p_{win})\,(U_{win}) + (p_{lose})\,(U_{lose})$ reflect the description that his state might win or might lose?

_____

_____

b) Say a state has a utility of 100 for peace, and a utility of 500 for winning, but losing is very bad, and so the state has a utility of –1,000 for losing. Say the state is equal in strength to the other side, so $p_{win} = 0.5$ and $p_{lose} = 0.5$. Should the state attack? (*Hint:* Compute the expected utilities and compare.) Why?

_____

_____

c) Suppose the utilities are the same as in part b, but that the state has undergone a military buildup. It's now much stronger than the other side, and the military leadership informs the leader that there is a 75 percent chance of winning. All other values are the same as before. Could the state rationally attack now? (*Hint:* Compute the expected utilities and compare.) Why?

_____

_____

CHAPTER 4

AN INTRODUCTION TO GAME THEORY

GAME THEORY: STRATEGIC FORM GAMES

Exercise 4-1. *The Prisoner's Dilemma in International Politics*
The prisoner's dilemma fits any situation in which the following conditions are met:

- two actors must make simultaneous decisions (or make a decision without knowing what the opponent will do or has done already),
- defection always dominates cooperation, and
- the preference ordering for *both* players is DC > CC > DD > CD.

We must meet all three conditions to call the game prisoner's dilemma; if the first two conditions are met but the preference ordering is different for each player, or the same for both players but different from the one here, it becomes a different strategic form game with different implications (see below). The prisoner's dilemma situation, though, intuitively appears very common in international politics—so important that your professor may well ask you to memorize it. Here are two examples.

Arms Control Negotiations

Table 4.1 presents a game that states face when they engage in arms control negotiations. You can think of the players as being the US and the Soviet Union during the Cold War, India and Pakistan, Iraq and Iran, or any other two mutually suspicious countries with a history of poor relations.

a) Go through the cells of the game and think about each outcome. What is the likely preference ordering for state A? For state B? (That is, what outcome does each prefer, and what is the ordering of CC, DD, CD, and DC?)

b) Write the ordinal preferences (4, 3, 2, 1) for each player in table 4.1.

c) What do we expect the outcome of the game to be? Draw in what each player would do in table 4.1 and solve the game for the equilibrium in pure strategies. Write the equilibrium in equilibrium notation under the game.

d) Which problem(s) of cooperation—coordination, distribution, monitoring, or sanctioning—does this game show? Briefly explain your response.

TABLE 4.1

Prisoner's Dilemma in Arms Control

A	B	
	Cooperate (C): Reduce Arms	**Defect (D): Continue Buildup**
Cooperate (C): Reduce Arms	Mutual arms cuts; both sides save money and maintain security	A is vulnerable; B gets military advantage
Defect (D): Continue Buildup	A gets military advantage; B is vulnerable	Arms Race; both sides spend money and gain no security

Trade

Table 4.2 presents a game that states face when they attempt to make trade agreements. You can think of the players as being the US and Japan, the US and China, the US and the European Community, or any other two countries that say they want to engage in free trade but are concerned that the other side might cheat on the agreement. (An example of such "cheating" occurred in 2003 when the US defected on its agreement with the WTO by raising tariffs on imported steel.)

e) Examine the cells of the game and think about each outcome. What is the likely preference ordering for state A? For state B? (That is, what is the ordering of CC, DD, CD, and DC?)

_____

_____

_____

f) Write the ordinal preferences (4, 3, 2, 1) for each player in table 4.2.

g) What do we expect the outcome of the game to be? Draw in what each player would do in table 4.2 and solve the game for the equilibrium in pure strategies. Write the equilibrium in equilibrium notation under the game.

h) Which problem(s) of cooperation—coordination, distribution, monitoring, or sanctioning—does this game show? Briefly explain your response.

_____

_____

_____

Exercise 4-2. *The Effect of the Number of Players*

Table 4.1 in *Principles* presents the prisoner's dilemma. There, Chris can cooperate or defect, while Pat can do the same. This leads to four possible combinations of action.

a) Now suppose that Chris and Pat had an accomplice, John. John is also caught by the police and he faces two options: to cooperate or to defect. In this case of three players, how many possible combinations of action can you find? List them.

_____

_____

_____

b) Now suppose that there is no accomplice, but that Chris has *n* possible strategies while Pat has *n* possible strategies. In this setting, how many possible combinations of action are there?

_____

_____

_____

_____

TABLE 4.2

Prisoner's Dilemma in Trade

		B	
		Cooperate (C) Reduce Tariffs	Defect (D) Impose New Tariffs
A	Cooperate (C) Reduce Tariffs	Increased Free Trade	A loses jobs because of reduced exports from A; B increases revenue from tariffs
	Defect (D) Impose New Tariffs	B loses jobs because of reduced exports from B; A increases revenue from tariffs	Trade War: exports decrease, jobs lost in both states, tariff revenues decline as trade slows

Exercise 4-3. *The Afghan Taliban's Problem in 2001*

In 2001, the US and its allies threatened to overthrow the Taliban government unless it broke with Osama bin Laden. Table 4.3 shows the Alliance's choices as the two rows and the Taliban's choices as the two columns.

What is the Nash equilibrium in pure strategies?

TABLE 4.3
The Afghan Taliban's Problem

		Taliban	
		Break with bin Laden	**Protect bin Laden**
Alliance	**Overthrow**	(-10, -5)	(0, 0)
	Not Overthow	(10, 0)	(-5, 10)

Exercise 4-4. *The Israeli Prime Minister's Problem*

Principles presented the interaction between Israel's and Palestines' prime ministers. They are assumed to be playing the game in Table 4.4

a) What is the Nash equilibrium in pure strategies? Is there only one equilibrium?

b) What is the Nash equilibrium in mixed strategies?

TABLE 4.4
The Prime Ministers' Problem

		Palestine's Prime Minister	
		Swerve	**Go Straight**
Israel's Prime Minister	**Swerve**	(1, 1)	(-2, 5)
	Go Straight	(5, -2)	(-10, -10)

Exercise 4-5. *Other Strategic Form Games in International Politics*

The prisoner's dilemma is just one particular game, which is defined by the preference ordering for each country being DC > CC > DD > CD. But we can represent many situations using 2 × 2 normal form games. Many of these games take on "cute" names like the prisoner's dilemma, chicken, or stag hunt, but they can also correspond to real-world situations.

Several steps are involved in analyzing any situation using normal form games such as the prisoner's dilemma:

1. What are the choices? What do cooperation and defection correspond to in the real world (for example, building arms vs. not building arms)?

_____
_____
_____

2. What are the preferences of leaders or states across DC, DD, CC, and CD? What would a leader prefer and why?

_____
_____
_____

3. Lay out the preference orderings as 4 > 3 > 2 > 1 (for example, CD > DD > CC > DC).

_____
_____

4. Write the preferences for both sides as payoffs in a 2 × 2 normal form game. (Assume in these games that both players have the same preference ordering. In real life this is not always true, but in some stylized cases like these it works.)

_____
_____
_____

5. Analyze the game for what will happen by looking for one or more equilibrium points.

_____
_____
_____

Chicken

Say that I am one of two drivers racing down a deserted road and you are the other. We are racing straight toward each other. Our friends are watching us to see who has more guts. I want you to swerve, while I keep going. If you swerve, you are a chicken, and I gain status among our peers. If both of us swerve, then it's an okay outcome, because neither of us gains or loses respect, and we both may gain some respect with everyone else just because we played. If I swerve and you don't, then I am chicken and lose status among our peers; I don't like this much. But if neither of us swerves, we are both dead and it doesn't matter (this is the worst outcome for both of us—better to be a live chicken than a dead duck).

This game was made famous in the 1950s by interactions (including several deaths) between teenaged males in the US, especially.

The preferences for the game are as follows: DC > CC > CD > DD.

a) Solve the game in table 4.5 for the Nash equilibrium as we did previously. (*Hint:* There are actually two possible equilibria.) Write the equilibria in equilibrium notation under the game.

b) Which problem(s) of cooperation—coordination, distribution, monitoring, or sanctioning—does this game show? Briefly explain your response.

_____

_____

c) What situations in international relations might fit this kind of confrontation? Think of a situation (a specific example or a kind of interaction) in which state preferences and interactions might fit those described.

_____

_____

TABLE 4.5

Chicken

		B	
		Cooperate (C) Swerve	Defect (D) Drive Straight
A	Cooperate (C) Swerve	(3, 3)	(2, 4)
	Defect (D) Drive Straight	(4, 2)	(1, 1)

Stag Hunt

Stag hunt is characterized by a strong interest in cooperation, as long as each actor is certain that the other is cooperating. But if you as a player see that the other side is going to defect for some reason, you would also prefer to defect. The story of stag hunt is that two hunters are hunting a deer in the forest. It requires the cooperation of both hunters to capture the deer, which can feed the entire village. Instead of cooperating, though, the hunters can choose to defect to capture a rabbit, which will feed only one family. Hunters prefer to cooperate and capture the deer, but neither wants to be left waiting for a comrade if he or she runs off to get a rabbit.

The preferences for the game are as follows: CC > DC > DD > CD.

d) Solve the game in table 4.6 for the Nash equilibrium as we did previously. Write it in equilibrium notation under the game.

e) Which problem(s) of cooperation—coordination, distribution, monitoring, or sanctioning—does this game show? Briefly explain your response.

_____

_____

f) What situations in international relations might fit this kind of interaction? Think of a situation in which state preferences and interactions might fit those described.

_____

_____

Deadlock

Occasionally, there may be so many conflicting interests between state leaders that cooperation is absolutely impossible, and leaders do not even want it. Cooperation will never occur in a situation of deadlock, even with repeated interaction. The preferences for the game are as follows: DC > DD > CC > CD.

g) Solve the game in table 4.7 for the Nash equilibrium as we did previously. Write it in equilibrium notation under the game.

h) Which problem(s) of cooperation—coordination, distribution, monitoring, or sanctioning—does this game show? Briefly explain your response.

_____

_____

i) What situations in international relations might fit this kind of confrontation? Think of a situation in which state preferences and interactions might fit those described.

_____

_____

TABLE 4.6

Stag Hunt

		B	
		Cooperate	Defect
A	Cooperate	(4, 4)	(1, 3)
	Defect	(3, 1)	(2, 2)

TABLE 4.7

Deadlock

		B	
		Cooperate	Defect
A	Cooperate	(2, 2)	(1, 4)
	Defect	(4, 1)	(3, 3)

Harmony

Occasionally, states or leaders have very few conflicting interests, and so cooperation is natural, almost a given. In such a situation, you may not care if the other side defects, and in fact you might want to cooperate no matter what it does.
The preferences for the game are as follows: CC > CD > DC > DD.

j) Solve the game in table 4.8 for the Nash equilibrium as we did previously. Write it in equilibrium notation under the game.

k) Which problem(s) of cooperation—coordination, distribution, monitoring, or sanctioning—does this game show? Briefly explain your response.

_____

_____

l) What situations in international relations might fit this kind of interaction? Think of a situation in which state preferences and interactions might fit those described.

_____

_____

Coordination

Often players have multiple solutions to problems of common concern, but they must agree on one solution. As a very basic example, consider driving. Everyone in society benefits from everyone driving on the same side of the road. It really doesn't matter if the norm is to drive on the right (as in the US) or the left (as in the UK), as long as everyone agrees. Preferences might be as follows:

The preferences for the game are as follows: CC = DD > DC = CD.

TABLE 4.8

Harmony

		B	
		Cooperate	Defect
A	Cooperate	(2, 2)	(1, 4)
	Defect	(4, 1)	(3, 3)

m) Solve the game in table 4.9 for the Nash equilibrium as we did previously. Write it in equilibrium notation under the game.

n) Which problem(s) of cooperation— coordination, distribution, monitoring, or sanctioning—does this game show? Briefly explain your response.

_____

_____

_____

o) *What situations in international relations might fit this kind of interaction? Think of situations in which states' preferences and interactions might fit those described.*

_____

_____

Exercise 4-6. *Hypothetical Confrontation between the US and China*

Consider the real-world situation of relations between the US and China over Taiwan. Taiwan has an ambiguous status with respect to independence. Most people in the West, and many in Taiwan, consider Taiwan to be an independent country. Others, including the leadership in China, see Taiwan as a breakaway republic that is actually part of the People's Republic of China. The US has been an ally of Taiwan but has a strong interest in maintaining and improving relations with mainland China. One interesting question to ask is whether the US and China would go to war over Taiwan if there were a major crisis. We can analyze this situation using a 2 × 2 game.

Assume that a crisis has begun over the status of Taiwan. China has threatened to attack Taiwan if it does not renounce its claims of independence. The US, in turn, has threatened to attack China if it attacks Taiwan.

Cooperation in this case involves backing down or offering some kind of concession.

Defection involves escalation of the confrontation by either side—using military forces to attack or refusing to give in—leading to a more dangerous situation.

TABLE 4.9

Coordination

		B	
		Cooperate Left	Defect Right
A	Cooperate	(4, 4)	(3, 2)
	Defect	(2, 3)	(1, 1)

DD would involve both sides escalating to a war. Trade and peaceful interaction between the US and China would end.

CC would involve both sides agreeing to negotiate, leading to a peaceful resolution of the crisis with the status of Taiwan still unresolved. Trade and peaceful interaction between the US and China would continue.

DC would involve the first state escalating while the other backed down, ending the crisis short of war but giving an advantage to the first state.

CD is just the opposite, with the first state backing down while the second escalated the conflict, ending the crisis short of war but giving an advantage to the second state.

a)   Speculate about US and Chinese preferences across the four outcomes. What is the preference ordering for each side? That is, think about whether the US would prefer CC > DD > CD > DC, or DD > DC > CD > CC, or something else, and why. Then, think about what preference ordering China would have. Briefly justify your choice of preference orderings: Why would the state want the outcomes in that particular order?

US:

China:

_____

_____

_____

_____

b)   Label the game in table 4.10 for the two actors, the US and China. Decide which actor plays the rows and which the columns, and establish what the actions "cooperate" and "defect" mean in this situation.

c)   Write the ordinal payoffs that fit the preference orderings in part a in table 4.10.

d)   Solve the game in table 4.10 for any Nash equilibria in pure strategies, and indicate it below the game in equilibrium notation.

e)   Describe the equilibrium your actors reach (or the equilibria between which they must choose). Does this seem reasonable given your intuition about the real-world situation?

_____

_____

GAME THEORY: EXTENSIVE FORM GAMES

Exercise 4-7.   *Solving Extensive Form Games by Backward Induction*
Figure 4.1 presents a game between the US and Japan over trade. Preferences for the US: The US prefers expanded free trade to the status quo and prefers the status quo to shrinking trade, which results from Japan taking advantage of the US. So for the US: Expanded free trade > Status quo > Japanese advantage.

Suppose a new Japanese government comes to power. It prefers no change in world trade, but does not want to take advantage of the US. So, its preferences are Status quo > Expanded free trade > Japanese advantage.

a)   Write the new preferences in the game in figure 4.2.

b)   Solve the game by backward induction. Show your work by marking the figure.

c)   Write out the full equilibrium for the game.

_____

_____

_____

TABLE 4.10

US-China Confrontation

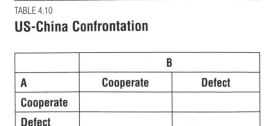

A	B	
	Cooperate	Defect
Cooperate		
Defect		

FIGURE 4.1

Simple Trade Concession Game with Payoffs

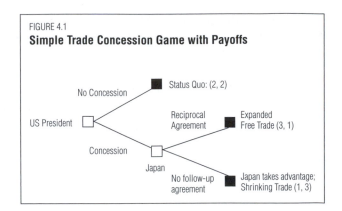

FIGURE 4.2

Unsolved Trade Concession Game for Exercise 4-7

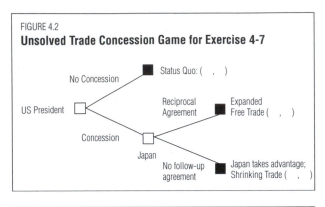

FIGURE 4.3

Unsolved Game with Cardinal Utilities for Exercise 4-8

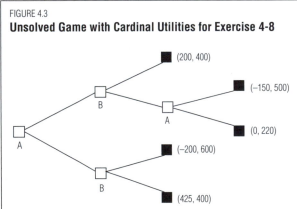

FIGURE 4.4

Unsolved Arms Control Game for Exercise 4-9a

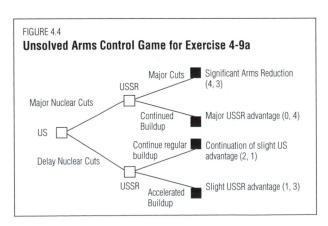

Exercise 4-8. *A Generic Game*

The game in figure 4.3 does not use ordinal payoffs (4, 3, 2, 1) but instead uses actual cardinal utility values (200, 400, etc.). Higher values are still preferred to lower values. (Game adapted from James Morrow, *Game Theory for Political Scientists* [Princeton: Princeton University Press, 1994].)

Solve this game by backwards induction, making sure to show your work by marking the tree. The game is more complicated than previous ones, but the same principles of how to solve it apply. (*Hint:* Remember in what order payoffs are written.)

Exercise 4-9. *Arms Control*

Countries often must decide whether to take a first step in starting arms control negotiations by offering a major cut to the other side. The problem is (as with trade) that the other country might reciprocate or might take advantage of the gesture. If the other side continues to build weapons when the first nation makes major cuts, it will achieve a potentially significant military advantage.

- Soviet Union: Major Soviet Union advantage > Slight Soviet Union advantage = Significant arms reduction > Slight US advantage.
- US: Significant arms reduction > Slight US advantage > Slight Soviet Union advantage > Major Soviet Union advantage.

a) The payoffs in this game (figure 4.4) are written with values other than the 1, 2, 3, 4 of prior games. Verify that the numbers used here are still ordinal and still reflect the preference orderings given.

b) Solve the game by backward induction. Show your work on the figure.

c) Think about what makes the two sides make their respective choices. Devise a modified preference ordering for the Soviet Union that would result in the two sides agreeing to significant mutual arms reduction. (*Note:* There may be more than one preference ordering that will achieve this.)

Soviet Union preference ordering:

d) Are these payoffs you posited realistic? Why or why not?

e) Write your new preference ordering for the Soviet Union and the original US preference ordering of the two sides in the game tree in figure 4.5, using ordinal preferences. Then show the backward induction solution to the game you have created in figure 4.5.

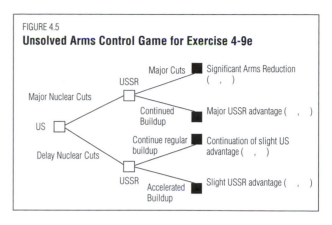

FIGURE 4.5
Unsolved Arms Control Game for Exercise 4-9e

Exercise 4-10. *Solving the North Korea–US Game with Uncertainty*

Principles added a move to the games in figures 4.4a and b. This move by "nature" assigns a probability that assigns a probability, R, that North Korea faces a US like the one in figure 4.4a and a probability, $1 - R$, that it faces a weaker US like in figure 4.4b. We can think about R and $1 - R$ as a measure of Kim's belief or perception about the toughness of the US president. Kim thinks there is a probability R that $1 - p - k = 0.2$ for the US. Moreover, he thinks that with probability $1 - R$, $1 - p - k = -0.10$. With this information in hand we can determine how big Kim must think probability R must be for him to accept a compromise rather than gamble on a retaliatory strike by the US. Kim's best way to work out whether to accept or reject a compromise offer is to calculate his expected payoff if he attacks and compare that to his expected utility from agreeing to a compromise settlement.

a) What is Kim Jong-Un's best response if $R = 0.83$?

b) What is Kim Jong-Un's best response if he believes that $R = 0$?

c) What is Kim Jong-Un's best response if he believes that $R = 1$?

d) Graph Kim Jong-Un's best responses as a function of R, where $0 \leq R \leq 1$.

Exercise 4-11. *Mixed Strategy Equilibrium*

Based on the games of exercise 4-5, find the mixed strategy equilibrium for Chicken and Stag Hunt.

WHY WAR

The Big Picture

Exercise 5-1. *Choosing War*

Consider again the case of negotiations between the US and North Korea over the latter's nuclear program, presented in chapter 3 of *Principles*. Suppose, as we did in chapter 3, that the extent of North Korea's nuclear program ranges from 0 to 1. The US ideal point is 0,[1] and North Korea's ideal point is 1. As part of the negotiations, each of the two sides can propose a position (call it x) that lies anywhere between 0 and 1 on the nuclear dimension. The larger x is, the more developed North Korea's program is, and the closer North Korea is to maintaining its current nuclear capabilities. Conversely, the smaller x is, the more nuclear facilities North Korea will have to dismantle. Ideally, the North Koreans would like to keep 100 percent of their nuclear program, or $x = 1$. The US, ideally, would want to see a complete dismantlement of North Korea's nuclear infrastructure, and thus the US ideal point is at $x = 0$. If the two sides fail to negotiate a deal, and resort to fighting, winning has a utility of 1 for the side that wins; the losing side gets 0. No matter the outcome, both sides pay a cost, k, for fighting. Assume that both the US and North Korea are risk-neutral, $U_{NK}(x) = x$ and $U_{US}(x) = 1 - x$, and that North Korea's probability of winning a war is p $(0 \le p \le 1)$.

Expected Utilities for War

a) Write an expression to show the probability of the US victory.

_____

_____

b) What is the North Korean expected utility for war? Write the complete EU expression and then simplify. Explain your answer on the line below (interpret the math in English).

_____

_____

_____

c) What is the US expected utility for war? Write the complete EU expression and then simplify. Explain your answer on the line below (interpret the math in English).

_____

_____

_____

---

[1] Chapter 3 of the textbook indicates that the US position on this issue falls between 0 and 0.25, and distinguishes between the ideal point of the Democratic Party (0.25), and the ideal point of the Republican Party (0). For simplicity, in this exercise, we assume that the US ideal point is 0, meaning that ideally the US would like to see no nuclear activity in North Korea.

Finding Acceptable Settlements

d) Let's consider the case from the North Korean perspective. According to the logic presented in chapter 4, actors should choose the option that gives them the highest utility or expected utility. In this case, then, North Korea should accept a settlement proposal of x if its utility is at least as much as the expected utility for war. Write an inequality to show this relationship. (Assume that if the values for the two options are equal—that is, the North Koreans are *indifferent* between the two—they will choose to take the sure thing, x, over the risky option of war. In other words, the sign should be "greater than or equal to.") Explain your expression on the lines below.

_____

_____

_____

_____

e) Assume for now that both sides will incur a cost of $k = 0.1$ for fighting. Solving your inequality for a range of p values will give you a corresponding range of x values that show you North Korea's minimum acceptable proposals for the current level of costs. Complete table 5.1 to find those minimum acceptable x values.

f) Graph your findings in figure 5.1. (*Hint*: Notice that the horizontal axis is p, North Korea's probability of winning, and the vertical axis is our outcome variable, which is x in this case.) This line represents the minimum x (proposed settlement) that North Korea should accept, given those costs and probabilities of victory. Shade the region of the figure that represents all acceptable agreements.

g) Now show the inequality for the US choices.

_____

_____

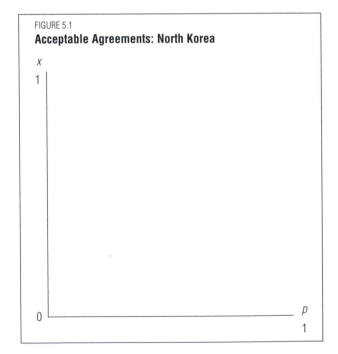

TABLE 5.1

North Korean Values for Settlement and War

p	k	Smallest x
0.1	0.1	
0.2	0.1	
0.3	0.1	
0.4	0.1	
0.5	0.1	
0.6	0.1	
0.7	0.1	
0.8	0.1	
0.9	0.1	

FIGURE 5.1

Acceptable Agreements: North Korea

h) As you did for North Korea, complete table 5.2 to find the US acceptable settlements for $k = 0.1$.

i) Graph your results in figure 5.2; label this line as k. Shade the region that represents all potential agreements that the US will accept. (*Hint*: Do the values of x that you found represent the *smallest* values of x that the US will accept, or do they represent the *largest* values of x? Think about what value of x represents the US ideal point.)

_____

_____

j) What happens if k changes? Select a new cost of fighting, k'; complete the k' and x' columns and graph your answers in a different color on figure 5.2. Label this line k'.

_____

_____

TABLE 5.2

US Values for Settlement and War

p	k	x	k′	x′
0.1	0.1			
0.2	0.1			
0.3	0.1			
0.4	0.1			
0.5	0.1			
0.6	0.1			
0.7	0.1			
0.8	0.1			
0.9	0.1			

k) Explain what happens to the line of acceptable agreements as k changes. Which way does the line move? As costs increase, do more—or fewer—potential agreements become acceptable? Why?

_____

_____

_____

_____

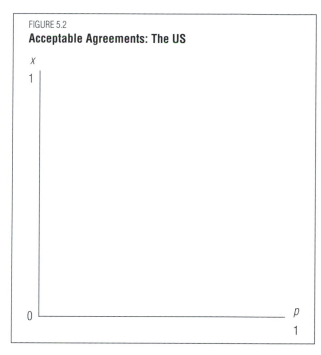

FIGURE 5.2

Acceptable Agreements: The US

More Realistic Assumptions about Uncertainty

l) Our earlier assumption that the two sides share a common set of perceptions about the likelihood of winning is probably not one that holds up in the real world. Let's adopt a more realistic assumption that the two sides have different perceptions of the probability of North Korea's victory (i.e., the value of p). Select one value of p for North Korea from table 5.1 above, and one value of p for the US from table 5.2. Note these values below figure 5.3 next to p_{NK} and p_{US}, along with the value of k (here, 0.1) and the corresponding x values for both sides. Next, use figure 5.3 to show the range of acceptable deals. Start by locating x_{NK} on the horizontal axis. Would North Korea accept deals to the left of that point or to the right of that point? Draw an arrow over (or highlight) the set of deals acceptable to North Korea. Repeat this process for the US: locate x_{US}, determine whether the US would accept points to the left or the right, and draw an arrow or highlight. (If you're highlighting, please use different colors and provide a key.)

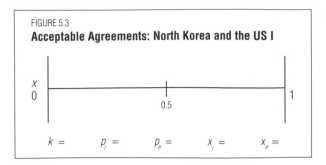

FIGURE 5.3
Acceptable Agreements: North Korea and the US I

$k =$ $p_I =$ $p_P =$ $x_I =$ $x_P =$

Do any possible deals exist in this picture? If so, where are they? How can you identify possible deals just from looking at the figure? If possible deals exist for you, indicate this set of possible deals—known as the *zone of agreement*—on figure 5.3. How large is the zone of agreement in this case, if you have one?

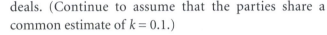

m) Let's repeat this process, but this time we're going to look for a case in which *no* possible agreements exist. Select a value of *p* for one party, insert this in the row below figure 5.4, and circle it to show that you're starting with this value. Complete the *k* and *x* values as well, and then graph your starting party's set of acceptable deals. (Continue to assume that the parties share a common estimate of $k = 0.1$.)

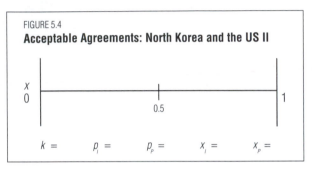

FIGURE 5.4
Acceptable Agreements: North Korea and the US II

$k =$ $p_I =$ $p_P =$ $x_I =$ $x_P =$

Now consider the table you made for the other party and consider what the figure would look like if no zone of agreement existed. Select, note, and graph a value of *p* for the other party that results in no possible deals. How do you know that no zone of agreement exists here? Given the value of *p* for the first party that you selected, what is the minimum value of *p* for the second party that will eliminate the zone of agreement?

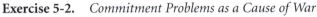

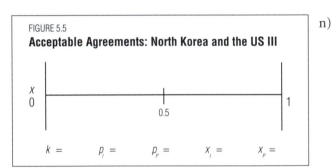

FIGURE 5.5
Acceptable Agreements: North Korea and the US III

$k =$ $p_I =$ $p_P =$ $x_I =$ $x_P =$

n) Consider a case in which the parties do share a common estimate of the probability of North Korean victory (i.e., $p_{NK} = p_{US}$). Find a value of *k* that results in no deals acceptable to either party. Indicate the appropriate values and graph your answer in figure 5.5. (*Hint:* You may want to make a table on scrap paper to experiment; if you do this, please turn it in with your assignment.)

Exercise 5-2. *Commitment Problems as a Cause of War*

Commitment problems occur when one side is reluctant to accept a deal because it fears the other side may have incentives to defect from the deal in the future. Several variants of commitment problems exist. The first, as *Principles* describes, is related to having a first-strike advantage. If a side can benefit from striking first at its opponent, then settlement proposals aren't credible. Both sides know the other will have an incentive to break the deal by striking first to capture more gains than it achieved in the settlement. A second variant involves agreements in which the settlement itself induces changes in the relative power of the parties. If the settlement in time *t* increases country A's power in time *t* + 1, then A has no reason to continue to uphold the deal after time *t* + 1. Now that it is stronger, it has the ability to demand more concessions from country B, and these concessions will make it stronger in time *t* + 2. Under these conditions, B should never accept a proposed settlement because A will defect from the agreement in the future. Finally, the third variant addresses the problem of disarmament. If A and B sign an agreement that includes disarmament provisions, both sides have incentives to cheat on that agreement. Disarming when you are unsure that your opponent is disarming as well would make you very vulnerable to defection by the other side. Upholding the deal here by disarming could be very costly: a surprise attack could leave you unable to defend yourself. This problem is most commonly found in civil wars, but it also may occur in interstate wars.

Let's consider the case of the Israeli-Palestinian conflict, discussed in chapter 5 of *Principles*. Assume that a deal to split the disputed territory has already been proposed. The Palestinians face a choice of whether to accept the proposed settlement or to fight. If they choose to fight, Nature then decides the outcome: the Palestinians win with probability p, and they lose with probability $(1-p)$.

If the Palestinians choose to accept the deal, Israel can either choose to uphold the deal, or it can renege (go back on the deal and use force to seize the ceded land). If the deal sticks, the Palestinians get x, and the Israelis get the remaining land. If Israel reneges on the agreement, then both sides use force and incur the cost k. Since the Palestinians have disarmed in response to the agreement, though, they are unable to defend themselves. They lose all of the ceded territory for sure in this case. Assume both Israel and the Palestinians are risk-neutral. What should the Palestinians do?

a) Draw an extensive form game to depict the situation described above. The game's payoffs should involve the variables x, p, and k.

b) As we've done before, we solve by backward induction. Starting from the right, we'll skip the Nature node for now and look at the Israelis' move. When will the Israelis choose to uphold the deal? According to the logic we learned in chapters 3 and 4, they will do so when their payoffs from upholding it exceed their payoffs from reneging. Write an inequality to represent the situation in which Israel will uphold the agreement, and reduce your expression to simplest terms. Then, on the lines below, explain the expression you found.

_____

_____

_____

c) Now think about a case in which the inequality is satisfied—that is, one in which Israel prefers to uphold the agreement. What is the Palestinians' utility (payoff) for accepting the deal in this case, when Israel prefers to uphold the agreement? Explain your answer.

_____

_____

_____

d) What about a case in which the inequality is not satisfied—one in which Israel prefers to renege on the agreement. What is the Palestinians' utility in this case? Explain your answer.

_____

_____

e) Now find the Palestinians' expected utility for fighting. Simplify as far as possible.

_____

_____

_____

f) According to the concepts we learned in chapter 5, the Palestinians will fight when doing so has a higher expected utility than settling does. Write the inequality that shows the Palestinians' expected utility from fighting versus the utility of settling if they believe that the inequality in part b of this exercise is satisfied and the Israelis will uphold the agreement. Simplify your answer and explain it below.

_____

_____

_____

g) What if the Palestinians believe that the inequality in part b is not satisfied and expect that Israel will renege? Write the inequality that the Palestinians would solve to determine whether to fight or accept under these circumstances. Simplify your answer and explain it below.

_____

_____

_____

h) Consider your responses to parts f and g. Why might the Palestinians choose to fight here, even when a deal is offered?

_____

_____

_____

i) *Challenge*: Would the Palestinians ever choose to fight even if they expect Israel to uphold the deal? If so, for what range of x, p, k, or combination of these would they prefer to fight?

_____

_____

_____

Exercise 5-3. *Negotiating a Water Dispute*

Suppose countries A and B share a common river that crosses from A's territory into B's. Every summer, country B accuses A of restricting the water flow, and denying B its share of the water. The two countries decided to settle the dispute peacefully, by trying to divide the water between them. B's leader announced that if these negotiations do not result in a satisfactory solution for his country, B was ready to go to war in order to secure the water supply. Let's normalize the amount of water to 1, and assume each country's utility from the water is equal to the share in its possession. Assume it is common knowledge that A will win with probability 0.6 if the two countries fight a war over this issue. Also assume it is common knowledge that war is costly for both sides, and A and B each have to pay a cost equivalent to 0.1 if they fight. A winner takes all the territory, and a loser gets zero. There are no other benefits or costs.

Assume that any negotiated agreement they reach will be implemented, and that both A and B will not fight if war and a negotiated agreement yield exactly the same expected payoff.

a) Specify allocations for which A and B would prefer to divide the water peacefully rather than go to war.

_____

_____

b) Provide a graphical representation of the issue space and the bargaining range from part a. Highlight the range of negotiated allocations that are unacceptable to A and B, respectively.

c) Challenge: Suppose A gets to propose a division, and B can choose only between accepting the proposal or rejecting it and going to war (the costs and the probabilities of winning are as specified above). Payoffs are realized directly after B's decision. What will A optimally propose? What choice will B optimally take? In this scenario, is there a first-mover advantage, a second-mover advantage, or neither?

_____

_____

d) Describe two reasons for which A and B could decide to fight in equilibrium. You can declare assumptions different from the ones used above, but make sure to explain how any such change is necessary in order for war to occur in equilibrium.

_____

_____

_____

Exercise 5-4.   *Stability in Multipolar Systems*

Create two international systems with the characteristics described below. List the states and their power allocations in the work space below the question. Then, on the lines below each system, determine if it is stable (in the neorealist sense of the word). If it is unstable, which states are inessential? If it is stable, identify the different blocking coalitions that could form.

a) Think of a five-state international system that has 100 units of power. Assign those units as follows:

State A: day of your birth (e.g., Valentine's Day = 14)

State B: sum of the digits of your house number

State C: sum of the digits of your current phone number (keep adding the digits until the number is less than 40)

State D and State E: divide all remaining units of power across these two states in any manner you wish

_____

_____

_____

b) Now think of a second five-state international system that has 200 units of power. Assign those units as follows:

State A: sum of the digits of your GPA

State B: last two digits of your student ID number

State C: the number of college credits you've completed (not counting the current term)

State D and State E: divide all remaining units of power across these two states in any manner that you
wish

_____

_____

_____

Exercise 5-5. *Essential and Inessential States*

Over time, quite a few once-essential states have disappeared, and other states have become essential. Below,
make a list of inessential states that have become essential or once-essential states that have become inessential and
have possibly disappeared. (Check Appendix A of *Principles* to brush up on history if you need some ideas.) Then,
look at your list and propose one hypothesis for why states become inessential and another for why they become
essential. Briefly discuss the logic behind your hypotheses and identify two or three cases from your list that fit
your hypotheses.

Became Essential: Became Inessential:

Hypothesis for becoming inessential:

_____

_____

_____

Hypothesis for becoming essential:

_____

_____

_____

Exercise 5-6. *British and US Hegemonic Norms*

a) Great Britain is often considered to be the hegemonic power of the nineteenth century. What rules or norms
of international conduct did Britain try to enforce around the world? (*Hint*: Consult Appendix A of *Principles*
if you need a history refresher.)

_____

_____

_____

b) The US is the post–Cold War hegemonic power or, in power transition terms, the state at the top of the power
pyramid. What are some of the rules or norms of international conduct that the US tries to enforce around the
world today?

_____

_____

_____

c) World War II is frequently interpreted as a failed attempt by Germany to replace Britain as the hegemon.
Think about a counterfactual world in which Germany won World War II and rules northern Europe and
Russia while Italy rules southern Europe and North Africa. The US has retreated back into isolationism.
Give several examples of *international* norms that might have emerged in a fascist-dominated postwar

world. (*Hint*: Think about the key norms of the postwar liberal capitalist hegemony of the US. What would be different?)

_____

_____

_____

_____

_____

Exercise 5-7.   *Proportional Reduction in Error*

A statistic known as the proportional reduction in error (PRE) helps us compare the empirical accuracy of different theories. Let's use a simple numerical example to explore this useful tool.

Brussels, Belgium, is a very rainy place. In fact, Brussels gets rain (or snow) about 300 days a year, leaving only 65 days of sun—or at least no precipitation. If you were asked to predict the weather in Brussels on any given day, your best guess would be to pick the modal (most frequently occurring) category: rain. About five-sixths of the time (82 percent, to be exact), you would be right. The other 18 percent of the time, you would have predicted erroneously. We call this prediction of the most common outcome the *null hypothesis*.

Another "theory" predicts a six-day weather pattern: rain, rain, rain, rain, rain, sun. Data show that this theory correctly predicts 322 days, or about 91 percent of the time. About 9 percent of the predictions are incorrect.

To calculate the PRE of our weather pattern theory, we compare the share of cases (days, in this example) we predicted incorrectly using the theory with how many cases we predicted incorrectly just using the null hypothesis. The null hypothesis, "the modal outcome occurs in every case," predicts correctly 82 percent of the time. Our weather pattern theory predicts correctly 91 percent of the time. The modal category, as we saw above, contains 82 percent of the outcomes.

The general formula for PRE is

(% correct by theory − % correct by null) / (100 − % of cases correct by null)

Inserting our values, we find

(91% − 82%) / (100% − 82%) = 9 / 18 = 1/2 or 50%

The weather pattern theory improves on the null hypothesis by making half as many predictive errors as the null. We have reduced our errors by 50 percent—hence, the term PRE.

Exercise 5-8.   *Measuring PRE in Power Transition Theory*

a)   What is the PRE (proportional reduction in error) gained from the power transition theory, as indicated by the evidence in table 5.3? (*Hint*: Determine carefully what represents the outcome, rows or columns, and which outcome occurs most frequently.)

TABLE 5.3

Empirical Evidence for the Power Transition Theory

Does War Occur?	Power Is Unequal	Power Is Equal and Challenger Is Not Overtaking Hegemon	Power Is Equal and Challenger Is Overtaking Hegemon
No	4	6	5
Yes	0	0	5

Source: Adapted from A.F.K. Organski and Jacek Kugler, *The War Ledger* (Chicago: University of Chicago Press, 1980), 52, Table 1.7.

b) Compare your findings to the results in table 5.2 in *Principles*. What should we infer when different statistical tests legitimately lead to different conclusions about a theory's explanatory and predictive potential?

_____

_____

_____

_____

Exercise 5-9. *Comparing Neorealism and Power Transition Theory*

a) Which assumptions do neorealism and the power transition theory share, and regarding which assumptions do they differ?

_____

_____

_____

_____

_____

b) How do neorealism and the power transition theory differ with regard to when wars are most likely to break out?

_____

_____

_____

_____

CHAPTER 6

DOMESTIC THEORIES OF WAR

Exercise 6-1.   *Threatening Country B*

In *Principles*, we observed how A's probability of attack depends on a threshold for p, the probability that A will win if A attacks B. In *Principles*, we also investigated how the probability of actually threatening country B depends on a threshold for X, the value of the status quo for country A. More specifically, if A believes that B will counter and A is prepared to fight rather than back down, then A threatens B, provided that its policy status quo, X, meets the following condition: $X < (1 + \psi) p + \psi (m - 1) - ka$.

Recall that Ψ measures the cost to a leader if she loses office. Ψ then measures the audience costs associated with the leader's choices in the game since loss of office is the cost the electorate can impose on a leader who fails to deliver the benefits they seek. The variable m measures the general domestic dissatisfaction with everything else the incumbent leader has done, including all of her previous domestic and foreign policies. The larger m is, the less competent the incumbent leader is judged to be. Ψ and m, then, are both domestic features in the crisis decision-making game.

a)   Assume that $\psi = 1$, $m = 0.8$, $X = .5$, and $ka = .3$. Use condition $X < (1 + \psi) p + \psi (m - 1) - ka$ to plot the probability that A will *threaten* country B as a function of p; remember that p is a probability. Interpret.

b)   Assume that $p = .3$, $m = 0.8$, $X = .5$, and $ka = .3$. Use condition $X < (1 + \psi) p + \psi (m - 1) - ka$ to plot the probability that A will *threaten* country B as a function of ψ. Assume that $0 < \Psi \leq 10$. Interpret.

Exercise 6-2.   *Bayes' Rule*

In December 2011, Kim Jong-un took over as leader of North Korea. At the time he took office, the world did not know much about him; this was particularly troublesome for the government of South Korea, as it wanted to know Kim Jong-un's potential approach to North–South Korean relations. In April 2012, North Korea launched a rocket, which was interpreted as a missile test.

Suppose that Kim Jong-un is either friendly toward South Korea, or unfriendly. Kim Jong-un had the option to launch the rocket or not to launch it.

a)   Use Bayes' rule to explore the probability that Kim Jong-un is friendly toward South Korea given that he launched the rocket (i.e., p (friendly | launched rocket)).

_____

_____

Exercise 6-3.   *Solving the IIG for a Pacific Dove vs. a Hawk Retaliator I*

Circumstance 1: Pacific doves can force opponents to back down. Sometimes a pacific dove can end up in a favorable circumstance when it initiates a crisis by making a demand. Consider the following situation between a pacific dove and the following particular hawk, which prefers to fight rather than capitulate (a hawk retaliator). This is what a pacific dove is hoping for if it makes a demand.

A's preferences are Acq$_B$ > status quo (SQ) > Nego > Acq$_A$ > Cap$_B$ > War$_A$ > Cap$_A$ > War$_B$.

B's preferences are Acq$_A$ > SQ > Cap$_A$ > Nego > War$_B$ > Acq$_B$ > War$_A$ > Cap$_B$.

a) Write in the payoffs that reflect these preference orderings for the two players in figure 6.1.

_____

_____

b) Solve the game in figure 6.1 by backward induction. What is the equilibrium outcome?

_____

_____

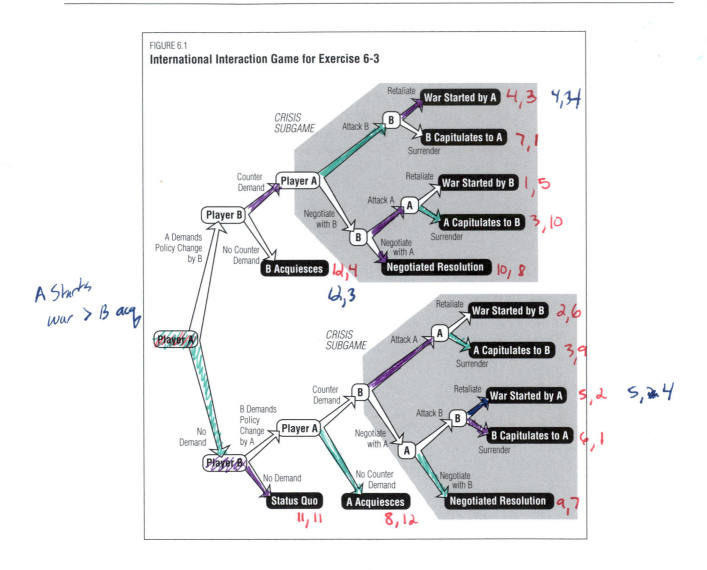

FIGURE 6.1
International Interaction Game for Exercise 6-3

Exercise 6-4. *Solving the IIG for a Pacific Dove vs. a Hawk Retaliator II*

Circumstance 2: In other circumstances, when a pacific dove issues a demand, however, it may be forced to back down.

A's preferences are Acq$_B$ > status quo (SQ) > Nego > Acq$_A$ > Cap$_B$ > War$_A$ > Cap$_A$ > War$_B$.

B's preferences are Acq$_A$ > SQ > Cap$_A$ > Nego > War$_B$ > War$_A$ > Acq$_B$ > Cap$_B$.

a) Write in the payoffs that reflect these preference orderings for the two players in figure 6.2.

_____

_____

b) Solve the game in figure 6.2 by backward induction. What is the equilibrium outcome?

_____

_____

c) There is one critical difference in the preference orderings in exercise 6-4 from those in exercise 6-3 that leads to this important change in outcome. What is it? Why does this one small change have such a large effect?

_____

_____

_____

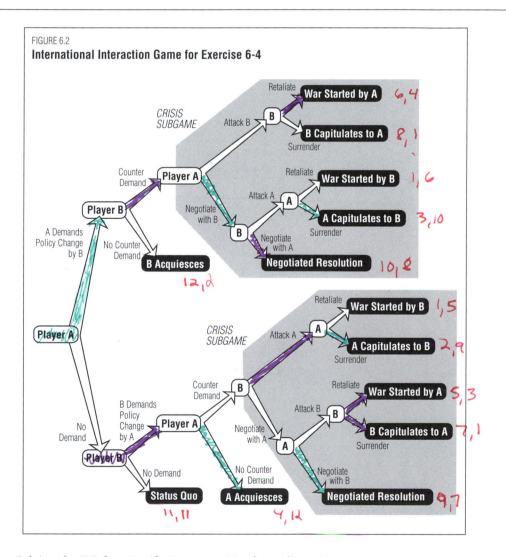

FIGURE 6.2
International Interaction Game for Exercise 6-4

Exercise 6-5.   _Solving the IIG for a Pacific Dove vs. a Hawk Retaliator III_

Circumstance 3: Sometimes, pacific doves may even find themselves in wars that they actually started. In this case, both states actually like the status quo as their second-best outcome.

A's preferences are Acq_B > status quo (SQ) > Nego > Cap_B > War_A > Acq_A > Cap_A > War_B.

B's preferences are $Acq_A > SQ > Cap_A > Nego > War_B > War_A > Acq_B > Cap_B$.

a) Write in the payoffs that reflect these preference orderings for the two players in figure 6.3.

_____

_____

b) Solve the game in figure 6.3 by backward induction. What is the equilibrium outcome?

_____

_____

c) Again, there is one critical difference in the preference orderings in exercise 6-5 from those in exercise 6-4 that leads to this important change in outcome. What is it? Why does this one small change have such a large effect?

_____

_____

_____

_____

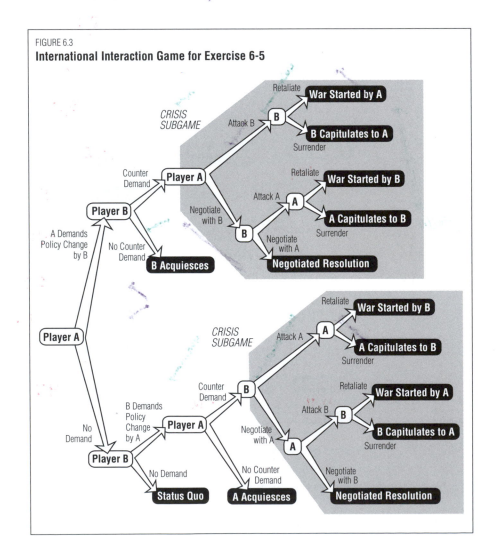

FIGURE 6.3
International Interaction Game for Exercise 6-5

Exercise 6-6. *Solving the IIG for a Pacific Dove vs. a Pacific Dove I*
In this case, both A and B are pacific doves that like the status quo.

A's preferences are Acq_B > status quo (SQ) > Nego > Cap_B > Acq_A > Cap_A > War_A > War_B.

B's preferences are Acq_A > SQ > Nego > Acq_B > Cap_A > Cap_B > War_B > War_A.

a) Write in the payoffs that reflect these preference orderings for the two players in figure 6.4.

_____

_____

b) Solve the game in figure 6.4 by backward induction. What is the equilibrium outcome?

_____

_____

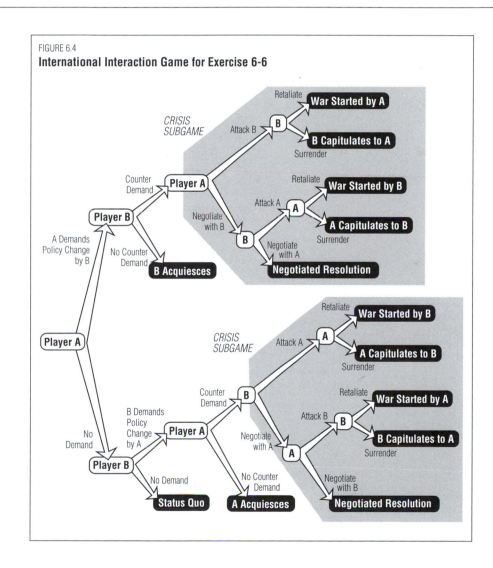

FIGURE 6.4
International Interaction Game for Exercise 6-6

Exercise 6-7. *Solving the IIG for a Pacific Dove vs. a Pacific Dove II*
In this case, both A and B prefer to negotiate rather than accept the status quo, and B actually prefers to force A to capitulate rather than accept the status quo.

A's preferences are Acq_B > Nego > status quo (SQ) > Cap_B > Acq_A > Cap_A > War_A > War_B.

B's preferences are Acq_A > Nego > Cap_A > SQ > Acq_B > Cap_B > War_B > War_A.

a) Write in the payoffs that reflect these preference orderings for the two players in figure 6.5.

_____

b) Solve the game in figure 6.5 by backward induction. What is the equilibrium outcome?

_____

_____

c) What changes in the preference orderings between exercises 6-7 and 6-6 lead to this important change in outcome?

_____

_____

d) Examine your work in exercises 6-6 and 6-7. When two doves are in a crisis, how do the outcomes differ from interactions involving a hawk and a dove? Two hawks?

_____

_____

_____

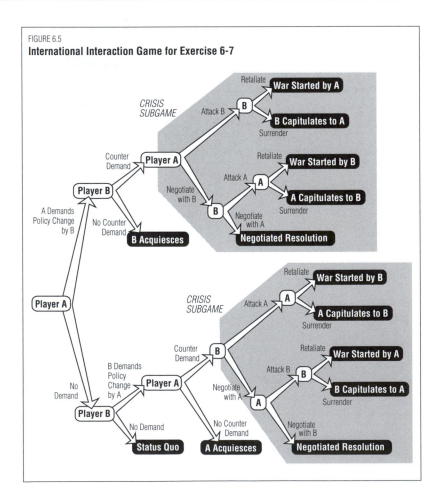

FIGURE 6.5
International Interaction Game for Exercise 6-7

Exercise 6-8.   *Resource Allocation and War Effort*

Suppose you are the leader of a country, and you have decided to go to war with a neighbor. You must now decide how much of your national revenue, R, you want to put toward the war effort. For simplicity, let's restrict the choices right now to all (100%) or nothing (0%). At the end of the war, members of your winning coalition will decide whether to reselect you for another period in office.

If you choose to put $R = 0$ toward the war effort, you will surely lose (which has utility 0), but you will still have all of your revenue to distribute to members of your winning coalition, w, as private goods.[1]

If you choose to put all of your revenue, $R = 1$, into fighting the war, you will surely win. Winning the war has a value V that is equal to some amount of public goods, v, plus some amount of spoils of war, r. Public goods are indivisible over the entire population, but the spoils are divided among the members of w.

Regardless of your revenue allocation decision ($R = 1$ or $R = 0$), war is costly. Each member of w will lose a *per capita* cost of war, k, as the cost of fighting. Because you are a strategic politician, you look ahead down the sequence of interactions; you know that you face reselection at the end of the war. By backward induction, then, the best choice for you at this resource allocation decision node is the one that makes members of w prefer to reselect you. Thus, we will focus on their payoff for war rather than yours, the leader's.

a) Write an expression that represents a member of w's utility for war if the leader chooses $R = 0$.

$U_w [R = 0] =$

b) Write an expression that represents a member of w's utility for war if the leader chooses $R = 1$.

$U_w [R = 1] =$

c) As a leader who wants to retain office in the next period, you prefer to put resources into fighting the war if, for members of the winning coalition, the utility of $R = 1$ exceeds the utility of $R = 0$. Write the equation that expresses this relationship.

_____

_____

_____

d) Consider the equation you wrote in part c of this exercise. How big does the public goods component of victory have to be for you to allocate all your resources to war? (Hint: Express your answer in terms of other variables and simplify as far as possible.)

_____

_____

_____

e) Assume that all of the variables in your equation are fixed (held constant) except for w. What happens to the value of the expression involving R, r, and w as w becomes very large? What happens to the value of that expression as w gets very small?

_____

_____

_____

---

[1] We use the small w here for convenience; this does not imply that your winning coalition is small.

f) For a country with a very small *w*, which side of the inequality you wrote in part d is likely to be larger? Given this, and given the preference of leaders with small *w's* to use private goods to reward members of *w*, are we likely to see a lot of autocracies putting their resources toward fighting in a war? Why or why not?

_____

_____

_____

_____

g) For a country with a very large *w*, which side of the inequality you wrote in part d is likely to be larger? Given this, and given the preference of leaders with large *w's* to use public goods to reward members of *w*, are we likely to see a lot of democracies putting their resources toward fighting in a war? Why or why not?

_____

_____

_____

_____

Exercise 6-9. *Exploring Relationships in the Resource Allocation Model*

This exercise builds on the expressions you wrote in parts a and b of exercise 6-8 and on the discussion in chapter 6 of *Principles*. You will need a ruler or a straight edge, a calculator, and several colored pencils, pens, or highlighters. For each section, evaluate the appropriate expression from above for the given values and plot the utility on the axes provided.

The Components of Winning: Values of *r and v*

a) Complete table 6.1 below. Evaluate the utility of your $R = 1$ expression from part b above using $k = 2$ and $w = 5$.

b) Graph the values you found in figure 6.6. For simplicity, the horizontal axis is v / v + r (the share of *V* that is public goods).[2]

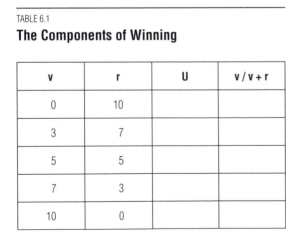

TABLE 6.1

The Components of Winning

v	r	U	v / v + r
0	10		
3	7		
5	5		
7	3		
10	0		

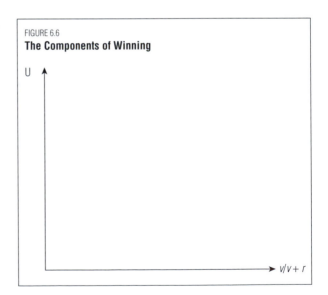

FIGURE 6.6
The Components of Winning

U

v/v + r

---

[2] If we didn't do this, you'd be trying to graph in three dimensions, which is not a lot of fun.

c) Consider the graph that you just drew. The line you plotted is a set of points. Why is that line useful? What do those points mean or tell us? (*Hint:* Think back to the expression you used to generate those points. What were you plotting?)

_____

_____

_____

d) What would happen to the line you drew in figure 6.6 if $k = 1$? If $k = 5$? Add these two lines to your figure in different colors. (Please provide a key for your instructor.) More generally, how do changes in k affect the utility of winning, and how does this appear on the graph?

_____

_____

The Cost of Fighting: Values of k

e) Let's see what happens now as the costs of fighting change. Consider again your expression from part b of the previous exercise, in which $R = 1$. Evaluate this expression in which $r = 4$, $w = 5$, and $v = 6$, for the values of k listed in table 6.2, and then graph your findings in figure 6.7.

TABLE 6.2

The Costs of Fighting: $R = 1$

K	U	$v' = \_\_\_ U$	$v'' = \_\_\_ U$
0			
1			
2			
3			
4			
5			

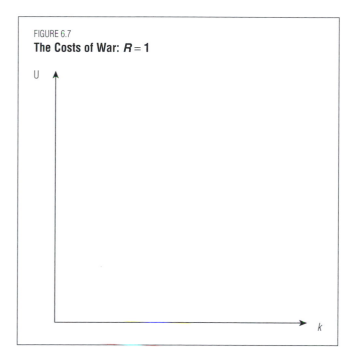

FIGURE 6.7

The Costs of War: $R = 1$

U

k

f) Now try the same thing using the expression from part a of the previous exercise in which the leader puts none of the revenue toward the war effort (i.e., the part of R remaining to be distributed to the members of w is 1). Continue to assume that $w = 5$. Evaluate the expression for the values of k listed in table 6.3, and then graph your findings in figure 6.8.

TABLE 6.3

The Costs of Fighting: $R = 0$

K	U
0	
1	
2	
3	
4	
5	

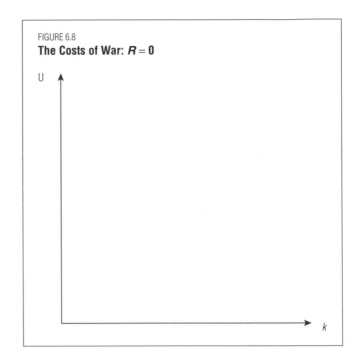

FIGURE 6.8

The Costs of War: $R = 0$

g) Consider your graphs in figures 6.7 and 6.8. How are they similar? How are they different? How does moving from $R = 1$ to $R = 0$ affect the utility of members of w?

_____

_____

_____

_____

Return to your graph in figure 6.7. How does the value of v affect the utility of war? Select two different values of v and note them next to v' and v'' in table 6.2. Then, substitute your new values of v and the listed values of k into the expression from part a of this exercise. Add these two lines to figure 6.7 in different colors.

i) Compare figure 6.8 and the revised version of figure 6.7. As v increases, does war become more or less valuable for a state that commits resources to war? Consider a state that doesn't commit resources to war ($R = 0$). What is the lowest value of v that can make the utility of war with resource commitment greater than the utility of war without resource commitment? Briefly discuss how you found this answer. Does your answer make sense? Why or why not?

_____

_____

_____

_____

Exercise 6-10. *Quasi-Democracies and Wars*

Two quasi-democracies, Russia and Georgia, fought a war in 2008 over the Georgian territory of South Ossetia. The territory is home to a large number of Russian citizens, thanks to forced migration in the early years of the Soviet Union. It is also a large portion of Georgian territory, however, and it is strategically located in the center of the country in a manner that makes ceding it to Russia (or allowing it significant autonomy) very danger-ous to the Georgian state.

The Data

Complete the data table (table 6.4) below for Russia and Georgia. You may wish to use the *CIA World Fact Book* (available at http://www.cia.gov), the country profiles provided by the UK's Foreign and Commonwealth Office (http://www.fco.gov.uk) or the US Department of State (http://www.state.gov), or similar sites to obtain some of your information. Use the following variable definitions:

- Who is in *W* and *S*? Identify major social or political groups.
- What is the size of *W* and *S*? Code this as small, medium, or large.
- Executive attaining office: This variable may have one of two values, selection or election. These terms are drawn from the Polity project, our most widely used measurement of democracy, and they capture the idea of "Executive Recruitment: Competition."
- Election: Chief executives are typically chosen in or through competitive elections matching two or more major parties or candidates. (Elections may be popular or by an elected assembly.)
- Selection: Chief executives are determined by hereditary succession, designation, or by a combination of both, as in monarchies whose chief minister is chosen by king or court. Examples of pure designative selection are rigged, unopposed elections; repeated replacement of presidents before their terms end; recurrent military selection of civilian executives; selection within an institutionalized single party; recurrent incumbent selection of successors; and repeated election boycotts by the major opposition parties.[3]
- Democracy summary: Consider all the data you reported in parts a–f of this exercise and summarize the level of democracy in each country on a scale of 0–4, with 0 being complete autocracy and 5 being mature democracy.
- Military size: Summarize the size of the military.
- Nature of dispute: Using the definitions and explanations provided in chapter 4, determine whether each side saw the dispute as one of an indivisible issue, a commitment problem, or a bargaining problem (involving private information and uncertainty). BBC News (http://www.bbc.co.uk) usually has excellent collections of articles linked together for any crisis or conflict.

TABLE 6.4
Comparing Russia and Georgia

	Russia	Georgia
Political Institutions: a) Who is in *S*?		
b) How big is *S*?		
c) Who is in *W*?		
d) How big is *W*?		
Executives: e) Who is the leader?		
f) How did the leader attain office?		
g) Democracy summary		
Conflict: h) Military size?		
i) Nature of dispute?		

[3] These definitions are taken from Monty G. Marshall and Keith Jaggers, *Polity IV Dataset User's Manual*. University of Maryland, College Park: Center for International Development and Conflict Management, 1999, p. 19. We thank the authors for permission to reproduce their definitions here.

Comparing the Cases

a) Consider your data table. To what extent was each leader constrained by his domestic audience? Briefly present some evidence from the case to support your claims.

_____

_____

_____

_____

_____

b) According to our theory about the effects of the size of W and S, which country should have been less constrained in its decision to wage war? Does the evidence from the case support this hypothesis? Briefly present some evidence for or against this hypothesis.

_____

_____

_____

_____

c) Consider the hypotheses about the democratic peace regularities and quasi-democracies. Which of our "regularities" from this chapter are supported by this case? Which are not supported? Provide some evidence from the case to support your claims.

_____

_____

_____

_____

_____

_____

d) Consider arguments about the causes of conflict that we discussed in chapter 4, which you've entered in your table as the "nature of the dispute." Which argument for the cause of the war seems best supported by this particular case? Provide some evidence from the case to support your claims.

_____

_____

_____

_____

_____

_____

CHAPTER 7

HOW INTERNATIONAL ORGANIZATIONS WORK, OR DON'T WORK

Exercise 7-1. *When Is Cooperation Easy—The Case of International Aviation*

It is easier to achieve cooperation in some areas of international relations than others. *Principles* mentions the common language used in air traffic control as an example of an area in which an agreement was relatively easy to achieve, and that enjoys a relatively high degree of compliance. A similar and related example is the standard for marking international commercial aircraft. An initial agreement about aircraft registration was reached early in the twentieth century, and the standard currently used around the world was formulated in 1944 in the Convention on International Civil Aviation. According to Annex 7 of the Convention, member states should notify the International Civil Aviation Organization (ICAO) of the nationality marks used by their aircraft.

a) Check which states are members of the Convention on International Civil Aviation (http://www.icao.int/publications/Documents/chicago.pdf). Then, check how many of the members have notified the ICAO of their nationality marks (you can check it here: http://legacy.icao.int/nationality/). What do you think of the compliance level with the requirements of the Convention? Why?

_____

_____

_____

_____

b) Can you think of a situation in which a member of the Convention would have an incentive to violate the nationality marking requirements, or take an advantage of others' compliance? How likely is this situation to arise?

_____

_____

_____

In addition to multilateral conventions, states negotiate and sign bilateral agreements that regulate air services between them. These agreements typically cover such issues as the routes airlines can fly, cities they serve, number of flights and number of passengers that can be carried on flights between them, ticket prices, and other issues pertaining to competition, safety, and security of air travel. You can learn more about bilateral service agreements on the following website constructed by the World Trade Organization: http://www.wto.org/english/news_e/news10_e/serv_14jun10_e.htm.

c) Based on the discussion in *Principles* (chapter 7), why do you think most air service agreements tend to be bilateral rather than multilateral?

_____

_____

_____

_____

_____

d) The ICAO holds annual Air Service Negotiation Conferences with the goal of expanding air service agreements, and promoting international civil aviation. Read the opening remarks of the ICAO's president at the 2011 conference (http://legacy.icao.int/icao/en/pres/kobeh/20111017_pres_speech_ican_en.pdf). Based on these remarks, what role do you think the ICAO plays in promoting air service agreements? How does this role differ from the role of other international organizations that you know?

_____

_____

_____

_____

e) The ICAO president in his opening remarks welcomes the inclusion of additional states in the process of air service agreements negotiation. He also expresses his hope that more multilateral service agreements would be concluded in the future. Do you think that the inclusion of additional states in the negotiation process promotes or inhibits the prospect of multilateral air service agreements? How would the inclusion of additional states in the negotiation process affect the content of a possible multilateral agreement?

_____

_____

_____

_____

Exercise 7-2. _Rivalry and Nonexcludability_

Consider the following goods, and for each one decide whether or not it is a rival good, and whether or not it is an excludable good. Explain your answer in one to two sentences. Determine whether each good is a private good, a public good, a club good, or a common-pool resource. Note that there could be more than one correct answer depending on the context, so be sure to provide a justification for your answer.

a) Military export controls

_____

_____

b) Tariffs on agricultural products

_____

_____

c) Dissemination of information about HIV

_____

_____

d) Women's rights

_____

_____

e) Cross-border oil fields

_____

_____

f)   Music property rights

_____

_____

g)   Free trade agreements

_____

_____

h)   National missile defense

_____

_____

i)   Greenhouse gas emission

_____

_____

j)   Malaria prevention

_____

_____

k)   Assistance in case of a nuclear accident

_____

_____

l)   Famine relief

_____

_____

Exercise 7-3.   *Collective Action Problem*

Consider two countries, A and B, that share a lake. The lake water is polluted, and needs to be cleaned up. Pollution prevents the lake from being used for tourism, and the two states lose potential revenue because their utility for the lake is 0 as long as it remains completely polluted. Suppose that each would derive a utility of 3 from having a clean lake. However, the lake can be fully cleaned up only if both countries participate in the effort. If only one country cleans up, the lake will be only partially clean, and each country's utility will be only 1.5 (including the utility of a country that did not participate in the cleanup). In addition, the cleanup process is costly, and each country that decides to participate pays a cost of 2 (regardless of whether the other country cleans up as well).

a)   Table 7.1 presents the four possible outcomes of this situation. Based on the description above, fill in the utility of each country in each of the four outcomes. Think about who pays the cost in which situation, and pay attention to whether the cleanup is partial or complete.

TABLE 7.1

Cleaning Up the Lake I

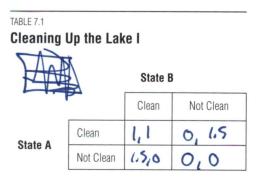

		State B	
		Clean	Not Clean
State A	Clean	1, 1	0, 1.5
	Not Clean	1.5, 0	0, 0

	C	NC
C	2, 2	-.5, 2
NC	2, -.5	0, 0

67

b) What is (are) the Nash equilibrium outcome(s) of the game in table 7.1? Explain why.

_____

_____

_____

_____

c) Do you think the public good of cleaning the lake is provided at the optimal level, underprovided, or overprovided? Do you think a free-rider problem is involved in this situation? If so, which state is attempting to free ride, and how does this interfere with an optimal cleanup effort?

_____

_____

_____

_____

In some cases, a public good cannot be provided unless a minimum number of participants contribute to it. In this example, suppose that the lake can be cleaned up only if both countries participate in the effort, and there is no utility for a partial cleanup of the lake. The rest of the assumptions remain the same: each state derives a utility of 0 if the lake is not cleaned, and a utility of 3 if the lake is cleaned; each state that participates in the cleanup effort pays a fixed cost of 2 (regardless of what the other country does).

d) In Table 7.2 fill in the new payoffs for each player in each of the four potential outcomes.

e) What is (are) the Nash equilibrium outcome(s) of the game in table 7.2? Does (do) the outcome(s) in table 7.2 differ from the outcome(s) in table 7.1? If yes, explain why.

_____

_____

_____

TABLE 7.2

Cleaning Up the Lake II

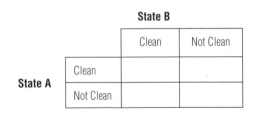

f) In some cases, states establish international, regional, or even bilateral organizations to promote cooperation in specific areas. For example, in 1991 Argentina and Brazil established the Brazilian–Argentine Agency for Accounting and Control of Nuclear Materials (ABACC) to promote peaceful use of nuclear energy. Suppose states A and B established an organization devoted to cleaning up the lake. What role could such an organization play in promoting the cooperation between A and B? How could such an organization make sure each state is participating in cleaning up the lake?

_____

_____

_____

g) How could a bilateral organization, established by A and B, change the states' payoffs, and make it worthwhile for them to cooperate? Amend the payoffs in table 7.2 to incorporate the role of a bilateral organization, and fill in the new payoffs in table 7.3.

h) Solve the game in table 7.3, and find the Nash equilibrium outcome(s). How does (do) the outcome(s) differ from those in tables 7.1 and 7.2?

TABLE 7.3

Cleaning Up the Lake III

		State B	
		Clean	Not Clean
State A	Clean		
	Not Clean		

_____
_____
_____
_____
_____
_____
_____

Exercise 7-4. _Repeated Interaction_

a) Consider again the game depicted in table 7.1. In chapter 4 of _Principles,_ you studied several well-known games that demonstrate strategic situations involving two players and that can be applied to situations in international relations. Which well-known game does the game in table 7.1 resemble? Why? (_Hint:_ Examine the preference ordering over outcomes.)

_____
_____
_____
_____

b) Suppose that states A and B played the game in table 7.1 twice instead of just once. Would the equilibrium outcome be different from the one in exercise 7-3a? Would it make a difference if A and B repeated the game 10 times? 20 times? 100 times? Why?

_____
_____
_____
_____

Infinitely Repeated Interactions

Let's suppose that A and B played the game in table 7.1 an infinite number of repetitions. A more realistic way of thinking about this would be to imagine that the lake needs to be cleaned up every year, and it is unknown when the cleanup will not be required anymore. As in exercise 7-3a, assume that the benefit for having a clean lake is worth 3 for each state, and that the lake could be partially cleaned if only one state participates in the cleanup. The benefit of a partial cleanup is 1.5 for each state, regardless of whether that state participated in the effort. The cost of participating in a cleanup is 2 for each state in every period in which that state participates, regardless of what the other state does or what that state did in previous periods. Finally, assume that each state discounts the utility of the next period at a fixed rate ($\delta = 0.96$).

c) Following the logic of the game in table 7.1, what is the temptation benefit (T)? What is the reward benefit (R)? What is the punishment (P)? What is the sucker's payoff (S)?

_____
_____
_____
_____

d) Using the formula for infinitely repeated summation of the reward payoff (R) presented in chapter 7 of *Principles*, calculate each state's payoff from always cooperating, if the other side also cooperates, based on the payoffs in table 7.1. Show your calculations. How does the payoff for cooperation change if we increased the δ? How would it change if we decreased the δ?

Grim Trigger Strategy

e) Suppose the states are playing a grim trigger strategy. Using the other formula of the infinitely repeated summation from chapter 7, calculate A's payoff for reneging and not cleaning the lake, if A knows that B is playing a grim trigger strategy, based on the payoffs in table 7.1. Show your calculations.

f) Based on your answers in parts d and e, do you think a grim trigger strategy is an effective tool to induce cooperation? Why?

_____

_____

_____

_____

Challenge: Now, let's consider whether grim trigger is indeed the best response available for B following A's defection. For this purpose, we compare B's payoff for using the grim trigger in response to A's decision not to clean up the lake in one period to B's payoff for ignoring A's one-time defection, and continuing to clean up the lake.

g) In the space below, use the payoffs in Table 7.1 to calculate B's payoff for using the grim trigger in response to A's one-time violation, and B's payoff for forgiving A and continuing to clean up despite A's defection in one period. (*Hint:* Think about how A would respond to B's use of the grim trigger strategy, and how A would respond to B's decision to forgive A. Remember that A is also playing a grim trigger strategy. You may need to adjust the formula from part e.)

_____

_____

_____

_____

_____

h) Based on your answer to part g above, do you think B can credibly threaten A to use a grim trigger strategy? Why?

_____

_____

Tit-for-Tat

In a tit-for-tat strategy, each player responds by mimicking the action of his or her opponent in the previous period. For example, if player A defects in period 1 while player B cooperates, then in period 2 player B defects while player A cooperates. In period 3 the players behave as in period 1, and in period 4 they behave as in period 2, and so on. The player who defects gets the temptation payoff, T, and the player who cooperates gets the sucker's payoff, S. The formula for calculating the total payoff for defecting once, and then playing tit-for tat is $T + \delta S + \delta^2 T + \delta^3 S + \ldots = T + \delta S$.

i)   Using the formula above, calculate A's payoff for not cleaning the lake once, if both A and B play a tit-for-tat strategy. Can the tit-for-tat ensure that A will always cooperate (clean up the lake) rather than defect once?

j)   Challenge: Adjust the formula you used in part i to calculate B's total payoff for using the tit-for-tat in response to A's defection. Compare this payoff to B's payoff for using the grim trigger and to B's payoff for forgiving A, and continuing to clean up the lake even if A defected for one period. Which option of the three is the best from B's perspective? Show your calculations.

Exercise 7-5.   *Commitment, Compliance, and Selection Effects*

Why do states comply with international agreements? States could comply, as constructivist and legalist perspectives suggest, because they feel a moral, legally binding or other obligation to do so. Other arguments, particularly those associated with the strategic perspective and neorealism, suggest that states comply because the agreement itself contains nothing more than a commitment to do what the states already intended to do.[1] The high level of observed compliance, then, is not a surprise: it is the logical outcome of this selection effect.

These arguments about why states comply also have implications for why states should sign an agreement in the first place. If the constructivist argument is correct, then states' identities should influence joining patterns. For example, states sharing identities should be more likely to behave the same way, with regional geographic identities ("we are [African/European/etc.]") and idea-based identities ("we are [democracies/liberal market economies/etc.]") being among the most likely candidates. In this argument, self-identification with a particular group brings with it norms of behavior that good members of that group are expected to follow. The selection effect argument, by contrast, suggests that we should expect to see states commit to a treaty if they are already in—or nearly in—compliance with the agreement. For a human rights treaty, for example, we would expect that current human rights levels would be a strong predictor of signing the agreement.

---

[1] This argument is most closely associated with George Downs, David Rocke, and Peter Barsoom, "Is the Good News about Compliance Good News about Cooperation?" *International Organization* 50, 2 (1996): 269–306.

Comparing the Arguments: Who Signs?

Tables 7.4, 7.5, 7.6, and 7.7 show data from research on why states sign on to, and then comply with, Article VIII of the International Monetary Fund agreement.[2] States that opt to sign this separate component of the agreement commit themselves to not placing any restrictions on their current accounts.[3] The variable for compliance with the agreement, then, is "Not Restrict"; the variable for defection is "Restrict." Let's begin by looking at the question of who signs.

Table 7.4 explains why states sign Article VIII by examining democracies and nondemocracies. The unit of analysis here—the thing being observed and counted in the cells—is a state-year: one year for a particular state. The scope of analysis is all IMF member states from their year of joining the Fund and all years from 1946 to 1997 for which data were available. The table asks whether democracy (the row, or independent variable) affects an observation's value on Article VIII status (the column, or dependent variable). For this analysis, a state is a democracy if its value on the widely used Polity IV democracy measurement is greater than or equal to the conventional value of 6 on a scale of −10 to 10. Both of these variables are dichotomous; they can take on only yes-no values. By convention, yes = 1 and no = 0. For this exercise, you will need two highlighters and a calculator.

a) Which school's argument does this table test?

_____

b) Eyeball the data. Do the data suggest that being a democracy influences signing? What makes you think this? (*Hint*: What does the theory predict about the values of the cells? What cells do you need to compare to make this inference?)

_____

_____

c) As you'll note from the bottom row of the table, the modal (most frequent) value of "Article VIII" is 1, that is, signing. Following the standard model of a proportional reduction in error (PRE) test, the null hypothesis is the most frequent category, signing. Highlight the cells of table 7.4 that show correct predictions by the null hypothesis. Then calculate what proportion of the cases the null hypothesis correctly predicts.

TABLE 7.4

Article VIII Signing and Democracy

		Article VIII		
		0	1	Total
Democracy	0	1,574	447	2,021
	1	914	1,410	2,324
	Total	2,488	2,857	4,345

[2] These data, and the arguments we examine here, are presented in more detail in Beth A. Simmons, "International Law and State Behavior: Commitment and Compliance in International Monetary Affairs," *American Political Science Review* 94, 4 (2000): 819–835, and Jana von Stein, "Do Treaties Constrain or Screen? Selection Bias and Treaty Compliance," *American Political Science Review* 99, 4 (2005): 611–622. We thank the authors for permission to use their data for this exercise.

[3] You might think of the current account as a country's checking account—it's the national balance for income (from exports) and debits (imports). Restrictions on the current account might, for example, limit access to foreign exchange to particular individuals, banks, or firms, or they might limit it by quantity of funds exchanged per day, or things like that.

d) Using a second highlighter in a different color, indicate which cells are correct predictions by our alternative hypothesis, which democracies are more likely to sign. Then calculate what proportion of the cases the alternative hypothesis correctly predicts.

e) Now, compare the null and alternative hypotheses by calculating the proportional reduction in error (PRE) statistic. Does the alternative hypothesis predict better than the null? If so, by how much? (*Hint*: See chapter 5, exercise 5-7, to review calculating PRE.)

_____

_____

Table 7.5 shows the same set of cases but instead explains signing behavior by looking at whether states were already at or near compliant behavior when they signed. We again examine all available state-years. The variable "Prior Restriction" indicates whether a state had restrictions on its current account in the year prior to the observation. Because this variable is lagged—that is to say, it takes on the value of the year prior to it—its value is missing for the first year that a state enters the dataset. This accounts for the smaller number of cases in this analysis.

f) Which school's argument does this table test?

_____

g) Eyeball the data. Do the data suggest that prior compliance influences signing? What makes you think so? (*Hint*: Which row indicates prior compliance?)

_____

_____

h) Highlight the cells of table 7.5 that show correct predictions by the null hypothesis. Then calculate what proportion of the cases the null hypothesis correctly predicts.

i) Highlight the cells of table 7.5 that show correct predictions by the new alternative hypothesis: that prior compliance leads to signing. Then calculate the proportion of observations that the alternative hypothesis correctly predicts.

j) Compare this new alternative hypothesis, H2, to the null hypothesis of the modal outcome. Using the proportion you calculated in part h of this exercise, calculate the PRE for the prior compliance hypothesis. Does the alternative hypothesis predict better than the null? If so, by how much?

_____

_____

TABLE 7.5
Article VIII Signing and Prior Compliance

		Article VIII		
		0	1	Total
Prior Restriction	0	554	1,344	1,898
	1	1,793	477	2,270
	Total	2,347	1,821	4,168

k) Compare your two sets of results in parts e and j of this exercise. Which argument is a better predictor? How do you know? How much does the better theory improve on the predictions of the weaker one? (*Hint*: Think about how we can determine how much better one theory is than another.)

_____

_____

_____

Comparing the Arguments: Who Complies?

Let's consider the issue now of who complies with commitments. Remember, compliance here is "Not Restrict." Table 7.6 explains restrictions on current accounts by examining whether states have signed Article VIII.

l) Which school's argument does this table test?

_____

m) Which variable here is the independent variable? Which is the dependent variable?

Independent = _____

Dependent = _____

n) Eyeball the data. Do the data suggest that signing influences compliance? What makes you think so?

_____

_____

o) What is the modal outcome in table 7.6? What is the new null hypothesis? Highlight the cells of table 7.6 that show correct predictions by the null hypothesis. Then calculate what proportion of the cases the null hypothesis correctly predicts.

_____

_____

p) Using a second highlighter in a different color, indicate which cells are correct predictions by the alternative hypothesis. Then calculate what proportion of the cases the alternative hypothesis correctly predicts.

q) Now, compare the null and alternative hypotheses by calculating the PRE. Does the alternative hypothesis predict better than the null? If so, by how much?

_____

_____

_____

TABLE 7.6

Current Account Restriction and Article VIII Signing

		Current Account Restriction		
		0	1	Total
Article VIII	0	598	1,890	2,488
	1	1,374	483	1,857
	Total	1,972	2,373	4,345

Table 7.7 explains restrictions on a state's current account behavior by examining states' prior compliance before signing. Again, the total number of observations is lower because of the presence of the lagged variable.

r) Which school's argument does this table test? _____

s) Eyeball the data. Do the data suggest that prior compliance influences compliance? What makes you think so?

_____

_____

t) What is the modal outcome in our new table? What is the new null hypothesis? Highlight the cells of table 7.7 that show correct predictions by the null hypothesis. Then calculate what proportion of the cases the null hypothesis correctly predicts.

_____

_____

u) Highlight the cells of table 7.7 that show correct predictions by the new alternative hypothesis, that prior compliance leads to signing. Then calculate the proportion of observations that the alternative hypothesis correctly predicts.

v) Compare this new alternative hypothesis, H2, to the null hypothesis. Using the proportion you calculated in part o of this exercise, calculate the PRE for the H2. Does the alternative hypothesis predict better than the null? If so, by how much?

_____

_____

w) Compare your two sets of results in parts q and v of this exercise. Which argument is a better predictor? How do you know? How much does the better theory improve on the predictions of the weaker one?

_____

_____

_____

TABLE 7.7
Current Compliance and Prior Compliance

		Restriction		
		0	1	Total
Prior Restriction	0	1,772	126	1,898
	1	139	2,131	2,270
	Total	1,911	2,257	4,168

Exercise 7-6. *Exploring Hypotheses about International Institutions*

Using your college's or university's library resources, obtain a copy of "The Rational Design of International Institutions," by Barbara Koremenos, Charles Lipson, and Duncan Snidal, from *International Organization*

55, 1 (Autumn 2001): 761–799. Skim the article and then use that information to help you determine where to read more closely to answer these questions.

a) Koremenos and other contributors to the special issue of *International Organization* (in which this article appears) define international institutions as both formal organizations and informal regimes. International organizations have observable characteristics: they have offices and budgets and staff. Regimes and other informal institutions, on the other hand, do not. If you were going to design a study to test some of the article's conjectures about rational design, you would want to include these informal organizations in the sample. What kinds of observable effects would informal institutions have? In other words, how would you know an informal institution existed so that you could include it?

_____

_____

_____

_____

_____

_____

b) For each of the international organizations listed below, identify two of the article's conjectures that appear to be supported by that organization's design. You may identify the conjectures as C1, M3, etc.; see the helpful list on page 797 of the article. You may need to do some background research on these organizations to respond. Helpful links are on the text's website at http://bdm.cqpress.com.

- The United Nations (UN): _____
- The Organization of Petroleum Exporting Countries (OPEC): _____

  _____
- The Organisation for Economic Co-operation and Development (OECD): _____

  _____
- The European Union (EU): _____
- The Association of Southeast Asian Nations (ASEAN) Regional Forum (ARF): _____

  _____
- The Shanghai Cooperation Organization: _____

Exercise 7-7. *Cooperation and Noncompliance*

a) We discussed in exercises 7-4 and 7-5 the fairly prominent argument that claims compliance with international agreements is high not because agreements are binding or because states fear punishment for defection, but because states will not sign agreements to do things that they do not already have interests or incentives to do anyway even without an agreement. If this argument is true, why might we still see noncompliance? Brainstorm two or three reasons and explain briefly why or how each might cause defection.

_____

_____

_____

_____

_____

b) For each of the reasons for defection that you identified in part a of this exercise, identify a way that states could mitigate that source of defection. Think about issues of institutional design like those proposed in chapter 7 of *Principles*, or those identified as independent variables in Koremenos et al.

_____

_____

_____

_____

_____

_____

_____

_____

c) Suppose you want to conduct research about the causes of defection you just proposed in part a. You have identified a set of cases of defection, and you now wish to identify which of your hypothesized causes contributed most to each defection. Consider your list of proposed causes. For each, identify one or two observable indicators that would exist or conditions that would be true if that particular cause were at work in a given case.

_____

_____

_____

_____

_____

_____

_____

_____

_____

_____

_____

_____

_____

CHAPTER 8

GLOBAL WARMING

Designing a Solution

Exercise 8-1.   *Natural Disasters and Political Survival*

Some scholars and practitioners believe that climate change and natural disasters are related. Natural disasters are particularly important because they have the capacity to kill thousands of people, destroy economies, and produce political instability. Two professors have studied the political consequences of disasters and find that countries with large coalitions protect their citizens much better from disasters than countries with small coalitions. For instance, figure 8.1 shows the number of people killed by disasters according to the size of *W*. This figure shows that countries with large *W* have a smaller mean number of deaths and smaller variance around it, while countries with small *W* have a larger mean number of deaths and a much larger variance.

Use the logic of political survival discussed in *Principles* to explain why countries with large winning coalitions experience less deaths from natural disasters than those with small winning coalitions. Make reference to potential control variables such as income and analyze under ceteris paribus conditions.

Exercise 8-2.   *The Necessity of Regimes I*

a)   See table 8.1. What is the single-play Nash equilibrium in pure strategies in this game? Write it in equilibrium notation. (*Hint:* See chapter 4 if you need a refresher.)

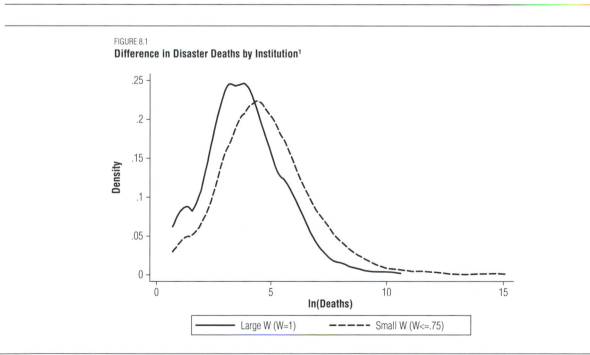

FIGURE 8.1
Difference in Disaster Deaths by Institution[1]

Density — ln(Deaths)

———— Large W (W=1)   − − − − − Small W (W<=.75)

Source: From forthcoming article by Alejandro Quiroz Flores and Alastair Smith, "Leader Survival and Natural Disasters," *British Journal of Political Science.*

[1]Adapted from Alejandro Quiroz Flores and Alastair Smith. "Leader Survival and Natural Disasters." *British Journal of Political Science.* Forthcoming.

TABLE 8.1

Game for Exercise 8-2

	B	
A	Cooperate	Defect
Cooperate	(3, 3)	(1, 4)
Defect	(4, 1)	(2, 2)

b) Can mutual cooperation (a CC outcome) ever be achieved in this game (possibly assuming repeated play)? If so, how?

_____

_____

c) Is a regime necessary, helpful, or irrelevant in achieving cooperation in this game, and why?

_____

_____

_____

_____

Exercise 8-3. *The Necessity of Regimes II*

a) See table 8.2. What is the single-play, pure-strategy Nash equilibrium in pure strategies in this game? Write it in equilibrium notation.

_____

_____

TABLE 8.2

Game for Exercise 8-3

	B	
A	Left	Right
Left	(4, 3)	(1, 1)
Right	(1, 1)	(3, 4)

b) Can mutual cooperation ever be achieved in this game (possibly assuming repeated play)? If so, how?

_____

_____

_____

c) Is a regime necessary, helpful, or irrelevant in achieving cooperation in this game, and why?

_____

_____

_____

Exercise 8-4. *The Necessity of Regimes III*

TABLE 8.3

Game for Exercise 8-4

	B	
A	Cooperate	Defect
Cooperate	(4, 4)	(3, 2)
Defect	(2, 3)	(1, 1)

a) See table 8.3. What is the single-play Nash equilibrium in pure strategies in this game?

_____

b) Can mutual cooperation ever be achieved in this game (possibly assuming repeated play)? If so, how?

_____

_____

c) Is a regime necessary, helpful, or irrelevant in achieving cooperation in this game, and why?

_____

_____

Exercise 8-5. *The Necessity of Regimes IV*

a) See table 8.4. What is the single-play Nash equilibrium in pure strategies in this game?

b) Can mutual cooperation ever be achieved in this game (possibly assuming repeated play)? If so, how?

TABLE 8.4

Game for Exercise 8-5

A	B	
	Cooperate	Defect
Cooperate	(2, 2)	(1, 4)
Defect	(4, 1)	(3, 3)

c) Is a regime necessary, helpful, or irrelevant in achieving cooperation in this game, and why?

Exercise 8-6. *Domestic Implementation of Regimes*

In *Principles*, we explored principal-agent problems. As explained in the text, in such cases, "We cannot be sure whether our leader is misrepresenting a situation for her own advantage or whether she is doing the best she can for us." Leaders often need their own agents to get things done; ruling a country is not easy and leaders need to delegate. For instance, once a leader has signed a treaty, it needs to be implemented in the leader's country. Take carbon emissions. If the leader has committed to get all national industries to reduce carbon emissions, he cannot personally observe each of these industries every day to make sure they reduce their emissions.

Now suppose that the leader of a certain country has installed a new device that monitors carbon emissions in the country's factories. There are only two types of factories: those that reduce emissions and those that do not. The device, called "CO_2," indicates whether the factory is cooperating and hence reducing emissions or not cooperating and not reducing emissions. Unfortunately, the device is not perfect.

With the device, the probability that the factory is charged with lack of cooperation is 3/9. The probability that a factory is charged with lack of cooperation given that it is actually not cooperating is 4/5. The probability that a factory is cooperating is 8/9. Based on the results provided by the device, a factory has been charged with lack of cooperation.

a) Use Bayes' theorem to find the probability that the factory is actually cooperating, given that the device indicates that the industry is not cooperating. (*Hint:* You may want to first find the probability that the industry is not cooperating given the lack of cooperation charges in order to find the probability that the industry is cooperating given the charges.)

Exercise 8-7. *Greenhouse Gas Abatement*

Principles discusses a prisoner's dilemma in which the US considers putting $50 billion aside annually to spend on greenhouse gas abatement in Brazil. The game is in a repeated—annual—prisoner's dilemma setting in which both the US and Brazil are democracies with regular elections and the shadow of the future is not very high for either government (i.e., $\delta = 0.80$ for Brazilian and American politicians).

How does the result of the repeated game change if the shadow of the future *is* very small (say, $\delta = 0.1$) for either government? You can describe the result with words, or use math to explain it.

HUMAN RIGHTS, INTERNATIONAL LAW, AND NORMS

Exercise 9-1. *Approaches to International Law*

The Syrian Arab Republic has been in the midst of a violent civil war since early 2011. The deteriorating situation in Syria, and the reports of gross human rights violations led the UN Human Rights Council to form an independent commission to investigate these events. Commission reports are submitted periodically to the UN General Assembly. Consider the following excerpts from the commission's first report, submitted on November 23, 2011:[1]

> 23. The Syrian Arab Republic is party to most major international human rights treaties, including the International Covenant on Economic, Social and Cultural Right, the International Covenant on Civil and Political Rights, the Convention on the Elimination of All Forms of Racial Discrimination, the Convention against Torture and Other Cruel, Inhumane or Degrading Treatment or Punishment, the Convention on the Rights of the Child and the Optional Protocol thereto on the involvement of children in armed conflict, and the Convention on the Prevention and Punishment of the Crime of Genocide. . . .
>
> 25. Derogations from human rights provisions are foreseen only in certain human rights treaties, and are exclusively permitted under specific circumstances. The Syrian Arab Republic has never notified the Secretary-General of any state of emergency and subsequent derogations made to its obligations under the International Covenant on Civil and Political Rights. Non-derogable provisions include, but are not limited to, the right to life, the prohibition of torture or cruel, inhumane or degrading punishment, and freedom of thought, conscience and religion. The commission furthermore recalls that article 2(2) of the Convention against Torture states that "no exceptional circumstances whatsoever, whether a state of war or a threat of war, internal political instability or any other public emergency, may be revoked as a justification of torture." . . .
>
> 84. On the basis of the information and evidence collected, the commission has reached conclusions with regard to a number of serious violations of international human rights law. . . .
>
> 87. The Syrian Arab Republic has violated the right to life, as enshrined in article 6 of the International Covenant on Civil and Political Rights, through the use of excessive force by military and security forces as well as by militia, such as Shabbiha, acting in complicity with, or with the acquiescence of, State officials and forces. . . .
>
> 93. The commission concludes that the extensive practices of torture indicate a State-sanctioned policy of repression, which manifestly violates the State's obligations under article 7 of the International Covenant on Civil and Political Rights, the Convention against Torture, and article 37 of the Convention on the Rights of the Child.

a) What does the constructivist approach predict with regard to states' compliance with international norms and laws?

---

[1] The full report can be downloaded here: http://www.unhcr.org/refworld/pdfid/4edde9d02.pdf (accessed August 22, 2012).

_____

_____

_____

a. Using online or other resources, find when the International Covenant on Civil and Political Rights, the Convention against Torture and Other Cruel, Inhumane or Degrading Treatment or Punishment, and the Convention on the Rights of the Child were concluded, and when Syria became a member of these conventions.[2]

_____

_____

_____

_____

_____

b) What does your answer in part b imply with regard to the constructivist prediction? Why?

_____

_____

_____

_____

_____

c) How does the neorealist approach explain the inconsistency between Syria's international legal obligations and its human rights practices?

_____

_____

_____

_____

_____

d) How does the selectorate approach explain the inconsistency between Syria's international legal obligations and its human rights practices?

_____

_____

_____

_____

_____

Exercise 9-2. *Human Rights as a Public Good: The Selectorate Theory View*

a) Consider the International Covenant on Civil and Political Rights. List at least five rights protected by this convention.[3]

_____

_____

---

[2] This information is available on the UN Treaty Collection website at http://treaties.un.org/Pages/Treaties.aspx?id=4&subid=A&lang=en (accessed August 22, 2012).

[3] You can access the full convention text here: http://www2.ohchr.org/english/law/ccpr.htm (accessed August 22, 2012).

_____

_____

_____

b) Using the definitions of public and private goods introduced in chapters 2 and 7, explain whether these rights constitute public goods and why.

_____

_____

_____

_____

c) Based on the selectorate theory logic, which political systems are more likely to join and are more likely to comply with international human rights conventions? Develop testable hypotheses. What is your dependent variable, and what is your independent variable?

_____

_____

_____

_____

_____

Exercise 9-3.   *International Law Acceptance as a Costly Signal*

a) Does international law reflect or change states' behavior? What are the positions of the neorealist, strategic, and constructivist approaches in response to this question?

_____

_____

_____

_____

_____

_____

_____

_____

_____

_____

b) According to the strategic approach, acceptance of international law creates a costly signal that constrains a state's range of future actions. What is a costly signal, and why do states need to send such signals (how does they differ from "noncostly" signals). How does acceptance of international law constitute a costly signal? Provide an example.

_____

_____

_____

_____

_____

_____
_____
_____
_____
_____
_____
_____

c) Are all international obligations equal in terms of the costly signal that their acceptance sends? Which provisions or conditions can enhance the cost of accepting treaties?

_____
_____
_____
_____

d) Which states or which leaders are more likely to face higher costs for violating treaties? Why?

_____
_____
_____
_____

Exercise 9-4. *Political and Economic Rights*

Chapter 9 in *Principles* highlights the following quote from the Vienna Declaration and Program of Action (1993):[4]

14. The existence of widespread extreme poverty inhibits the full and effective enjoyment of human rights.

a) What does this quote imply with regard to which states are more likely to enjoy good human rights practices?

_____
_____

b) If we consider this statement in terms of the scientific method, what does the statement imply about what is the dependent variable and what is the independent variable?

_____
_____

c) Do you think this is a testable proposition? Is it falsifiable? What evidence would falsify this claim?

_____
_____

d) Propose a research design to test this claim. Which cases would you include? What data do you need to measure your variables and perform this test?

_____
_____

_____

[4] The full text of the declaration is available here: http://www.unhcr.org/refworld/pdfid/3ae6b39ec.pdf (accessed August 22, 2012).

_____

_____

_____

Suppose you find that poverty is indeed highly correlated with bad human rights practices. Provide at least three different explanations for this hypothetical finding.

_____

_____

_____

_____

Exercise 9-5. *Democracy, Freedom, and Economic Development: An Experiment with Data*

The World Bank website provides data on numerous indicators that can help us explore the social and economic development of different countries. We will use this data source, and combine it with the Polity IV and Freedom House datasets to investigate the relationship between political and economic development. The World Bank indicators data can be accessed at http://data.worldbank.org/topic, the Polity IV dataset at http://www.systemicpeace.org/polity/polity4.htm, and the Freedom House rankings at http://www.freedomhouse.org/report-types/freedom-world.

a) On the World Bank website, click on "Economic Policy and External Debt," and find "GDP per capita (current US$)." This indicator measures the average annual income per capita in current US dollars. Higher income indicates lower poverty, and lower income is associated with higher poverty. Click on the up arrow next to the year 2010 to sort the countries in descending order by per capita income. In tables 9.1a and b below, list the top 10 and bottom 10 states, respectively, according to their per capita income in 2010, from the wealthiest to the poorest in each group.

_____

_____

b) Go to the Polity IV website, and scroll down to "Polity IV Individual Country Regime Trends, 1946-2010." Next to each state in tables 9.1a and b, record that state's polity score in 2010. If a state you identified does not have a polity score (this might be the case for very small states), then omit it from your list, and add the next state in the per capita income ranking that has a polity score. Also, omit states for which the per capita income data are missing. Remember, the polity score ranges from −10 to +10, with higher scores indicating higher levels of democracy. States are usually considered democratic if they have a polity score of 6 or above. According to your data, is there a relationship between per capita income and regime type? If yes, then is democracy positively or negatively correlated with per capita income?

_____

_____

_____

_____

c) Go to the Freedom House website, and download the "Country ratings and status, FIW 1973-2012 (EXCEL)" file. In tables 9.1a and b, record the political rights (PR) and the civil liberties (CL) scores of the top 10 and bottom 10 countries by per capita income. Note that the PR and the CL range from 1 to 7, with lower numbers indicating more political rights and more civil liberties. According to your data, does a relationship exist

TABLE 9.1A

Poverty and Political Regimes—Top 10 States

Rank	Top 10 Income per Capita States in 2010 (in descending order from the wealthiest to the poorest)	Polity Score in 2010	Political Rights (PR) in 2010	Civil Liberties (CL) in 2010
1				
2				
3				
4				
5				
6				
7				
8				
9				
10				

TABLE 9.1B

Poverty and Political Regimes—Bottom 10 States

Rank	Bottom 10 Income per Capita States in 2010 (in descending order from the wealthiest to the poorest)	Polity Score in 2010	Political Rights (PR) in 2010	Civil Liberties (CL) in 2010
1				
2				
3				
4				
5				
6				
7				
8				
9				
10				

among political rights, civil liberties, and per capita income? If yes, then is higher income positively or negatively correlated with political rights and civil liberties?

_____

_____

_____

_____

_____

d) If you think a relationship exists among per capita income, political regime, and political and civil rights and liberties, what possible explanations could there be for this correlation?

_____

_____

_____

_____

_____

e) Consider the case of Benin. Briefly summarize the political regime changes in Benin from 1980 onward using the Polity IV country graphs.

_____

_____

_____

_____

_____

f) Describe the changes in the Freedom House's PR and the CL scores for Benin from 1980 onward. Compare the changes in the PR and CL scores to the changes in the polity score you identified in part e. Do you see a trend? Are these scores correlated?

_____

_____

_____

_____

_____

_____

g) We will now use the three data sources to examine the relationship between poverty alleviation and democratization in Benin. Specifically, we want to know whether democratization was preceded by an increase in per capita income. Note that we are looking at only one country, so we can draw conclusions only about the relationship between these variables in the Benin context. Chapter 9 in *Principles* presents a cross-national analysis that allows us make more general arguments about the link between poverty and democracy. We will use data for six years: 1985, 1990, 1995, 2000, 2005, and 2010. For each of these years, we will compare the change in the GDP per capita in Benin from five years before $(t-5)$ to one year before $(t-1)$, to the change in the polity score from four years ago $(t-4)$ to that year (t). For example, for the year 1985 $(t=1985)$, we compare the difference in the GDP per capita from 1980 $(t-5)$ to 1984 $(t-1)$ to the difference in the polity score from 1981 $(t-4)$ to 1985 (t). The values for 1985 already appear in table 9.2. Fill in the values for the remaining years.

_____

h) Compare columns (6) and (7) in table 9.2. Do the data from Benin support the argument that alleviation of poverty leads to democratization? Why?

_____

_____

_____

i) Now let's ask the following question: does an expansion of political rights and civil liberties lead to democratization? As before, we limit our conclusions to the case of Benin. In table 9.3, fill in the data using the Freedom House dataset. Copy the data on polity scores from table 9.2 to table 9.3.

_____

_____

TABLE 9.2

Poverty and Political Regime

(1)	(2)	(3)	(4)	(5)	(6)	(7)
Year (t)	Polity$_t$	Polity$_{t-4}$	GDP per Capita$_{t-1}$	GDP per Capita$_{t-5}$	Change in Polity (2) − (3)	Change in GDP per Capita (4) − (5)
1985	−7	−7	261	389	0	−128
1990						
1995						
2000						
2005						
2010						

TABLE 9.3
Political Freedoms and Political Regime

(1)	(2)	(3)	(4)	(5)	(6)	(7)	(8)	(9)	(10)
Year (t)	Polity$_t$	Polity$_{t-4}$	PR$_{t-1}$	PR$_{t-5}$	CL$_{t-1}$	CL$_{t-5}$	Change in Polity (2) – (3)	Change in PR (4) – (5)	Change in CL (6) – (7)
1985	–7	–7	7	7	7	6	0	0	1
1990									
1995									
2000									
2005									
2010									

j) Compare columns (8) and (9), and columns (8) and (10). Do the data from Benin support the argument that expansion of political rights and civil liberties leads to democratization?

_____

_____

_____

k) Next, let's look at whether an increase in income per capita in Benin led to an improvement in political rights and civil liberties. We repeat the exercise in part i, only now political rights and civil liberties are our dependent variable. You can copy the data on GDP per capita from table 9.2, and use the Freedom House dataset to fill in the values for PR and CL in table 9.4.

_____

_____

TABLE 9.4
Poverty and Political Freedoms

(1)	(2)	(3)	(4)	(5)	(6)	(7)	(8)	(9)	(10)
Year (t)	PR$_t$	PR$_{t-4}$	CL$_t$	CL$_{t-4}$	GDP per Capita$_{t-1}$	GDP per Capita$_{t-5}$	Change in PR (2) – (3)	Change in CL (4) – (5)	Change in GDP per Capita (6) – (7)
1985	7	7	7	6	261	389	0	1	–128
1990									
1995									
2000									
2005									
2010									

l)   Based on the data you collected and summarized in table 9.4, how do changes in per capita income affect political rights and civil liberties? Based on the Benin example, can you argue that poverty alleviation is necessary for an expansion of political rights and civil liberties? Is it also sufficient? Why yes or why not?

_____

_____

_____

m) Finally, let's flip the previous question and ask whether an expansion of political rights and civil liberties in Benin led to an increase in per capita income. You can copy the values of PR and CL from table 9.3 to table 9.5.

_____

n)   Based on your data in table 9.5, what does the Benin case imply regarding the effect of expanding the political rights and civil liberties on poverty? Is the improvement in human rights necessary for poverty alleviation? Is it sufficient? Why yes or why not?

_____

_____

_____

_____

_____

_____

TABLE 9.5

Political Freedoms and Poverty

(1)	(2)	(3)	(4)	(5)	(6)	(7)	(8)	(9)	(10)
Year (t)	GDP per Capita$_t$	GDP per Capita$_{t-4}$	PR$_{t-1}$	PR$_{t-5}$	CL$_{t-1}$	CL$_{t-5}$	Change in GDP per Capita (2) − (3)	Change in PR (4) − (5)	Change in CL (6) − (7)
1985	253	348	7	7	7	6	−95	0	1
1990									
1995									
2000									
2005									
2010									

Exercise 9-6.   *Do International Treaties Improve Human Rights? The Case of CEDAW*

The Convention on the Elimination of All Forms of Discrimination against Women (CEDAW) was adopted in 1979. The purpose of the convention is to promote equality between men and women, and abolish discriminatory laws and practices "in the political, economic, social, cultural, civil or any other field."[5] Countries that have ratified the convention are legally obliged to incorporate it into their domestic laws, and enforce its provisions. They are also committed to submit national reports at least every four years on the steps they have taken to implement the CEDAW.

One important question is whether state parties to the CEDAW experience an improvement in women's rights following their accession to the treaty. The World Bank dataset that we use in exercise 9-5 also provides indicators related to women's status in various countries across time, and we can use these data to examine the effect of membership in the CEDAW on women's rights in different areas, for example, in politics.

_____

[5] The full text of the CEDAW, as well as the list of member states, and the dates of their accession, are available at http://www.un.org/women watch/daw/cedaw/ (accessed August 23, 2012).

a) Examine the list of CEDAW members (available at http://www.un.org/womenwatch/daw/cedaw/states.htm), and randomly select 15 countries that ratified the convention before 1997. Write down their names and the ratification year in table 9.6.

b) On the World Bank website (http://data.worldbank.org/topic), click on the "Gender" section, and find "Proportion of seats held by women in national parliaments." For the 15 countries you selected in part a, record the share of women among parliament members in 1997 and 2007. If the data for the state you selected are missing, randomly select another country until you have a list of 15 CEDAW members that joined prior to 1997, and their shares of female parliamentarians in 1997 and 2007.

c) Examine the data in table 9.6. Does it appear that the CEDAW member states have increased female representation in their parliaments between 1997 and 2007?

TABLE 9.6

Does CEDAW Membership Promote Women in Politics?

Country Name	Year Ratified CEDAW	Parliament Seats Held by Women in 1997 (%)	Parliament Seats Held by Women in 2007 (%)	Number of Country Reports Submitted

d) Are states that joined the CEDAW earlier more likely to have higher shares of female representation in their legislatures than states that joined later?

_____

_____

_____

_____

_____

e) The US signed but has not ratified the CEDAW. Look at the female representation in the US in 1997 and 2007, and add the US to your table. Does the US differ from the 15 CEDAW members in the rate of female representation in the legislature, both in terms of the share of women, as well as in the change from 1997 to 2007?

_____

_____

_____

_____

_____

f) Look at the data on country reports (available at http://www.un.org/womenwatch/daw/cedaw/reports.htm). Count the number of reports that the 15 member states submitted since their ratification of the treaty, and add them to table 9.6. How many of them have not submitted a single report since ratification? Examine the status of submission and consideration of reports. How many of them have not complied with the requirement to submit a report at least once every four years?

_____

_____

_____

_____

_____

g) Based on the data in table 9.6, and your answer in part e, how would you assess the extent of compliance of member states with the CEDAW?

_____

_____

_____

_____

_____

h) Suppose that all 15 of the member states you examined were in good standing in terms of their compliance with the CEDAW, and had a high share of women representatives in their parliaments. Could you interpret this as evidence that the CEDAW improved the status of women? Why yes or why not?

_____

_____

_____

CHAPTER 10

FREE TRADE OR FAIR

The Domestic Politics of Tariffs

Exercise 10-1. *Free Trade in Widgets and Gizmos*
   Table 10.1 indicates the productivity (the amount of output produced by one worker per day) of two countries (Malistan and Ukralia) for two particular goods (widgets and gizmos). Assume these are the only two countries that can trade these items with each other. Answer the questions below using this table.

a) Which country has an absolute advantage in producing widgets?

_____

b) Which country has an absolute advantage in producing gizmos?

_____

c) Which country has a comparative advantage in producing widgets?

_____

TABLE 10.1

Free Trade in Widgets and Gizmos

	Malistan	Ukralia
Widget	8 widgets/day	6 widgets/day
Gizmo	10 gizmos/day	20 gizmos/day

d) Which country has a comparative advantage in producing gizmos?

_____

e) Under free trade, which country would produce widgets?

_____

f) Under free trade, which country would produce gizmos?

_____

Exercise 10-2. *Free Trade in Bells and Whistles*
   Table 10.2 indicates the productivity (the amount of output produced by one worker per day) of two other countries, Zaioff and Lundikistan, for two particular goods (bells and whistles). Assume these are the only two countries that can trade these items with each other. Answer the questions below using this table.

a) Which country has an absolute advantage in producing bells?

_____

b) Which country has an absolute advantage in producing whistles?

_____

TABLE 10.2

Free Trade in Bells and Whistles

	Zaioff	Lundikistan
Bell	8 bells/day	4 bells/day
Whistle	12 whistles/day	4 whistles/day

c) Which country has a comparative advantage in producing bells?

_____

d) Which country has a comparative advantage in producing whistles?

_____

e) Under free trade, which country would produce bells?

_____

f) Under free trade, which country would produce whistles?

_____

Exercise 10-3. *Opportunity Cost*

Rare earths are crucial for the manufacturing of electronic devices such as the iPhone. These minerals are called rare earths not because they are difficult to find but because they are difficult to find in a single place to make extraction profitable. China is one of the countries that has large deposits of rare earths, making it one of the most important exporters of these minerals. Recently, Malaysia discovered large deposits of rare earths and is looking to extract them and compete with China in this market. Of course, Malaysia may choose not to implement this policy of extraction and concentrate on producing other goods.

a) How does the discovery of such minerals change the opportunity cost for Malaysia in terms of the production of rare earths? And for China?

_____

b) How does the opportunity of cost for Malaysia change if there is a massive increase in the demand for electronic devices that require rare earths?

Exercise 10-4. *Trade Restrictions I*

Assume that the US and Germany are trading partners. Assume further that in some year Germany exported 100,000 cars to the US at a price of US$30,000 each. But then the US placed a quota on imported cars from Germany, limiting the number to 75,000 per year.

a) What happens to the price of German cars in the US? Why?

_____

_____

b) What happens to the volume of imported cars from Germany? Why?

_____

_____

c) What happens to sales of domestic cars in the US? Why?

_____

_____

d) Who in the US is hurt by this decision? Why?

_____

_____

e) Who in the US benefits from this decision? Why?

_____

_____

f)   Who in Germany is hurt by this decision? Why?

_____

_____

Exercise 10-5.   *Trade Restrictions II*

Assume that the US and Germany are trading partners. Assume further that in some year Germany exported 100,000 cars to the US at a price of US$30,000 each. But then the US places a 10 percent tariff on cars imported from Germany.

a)   What happens to the price of German cars in the US? Why?

_____

_____

b)   What happens to the volume of imported cars from Germany? Why?

_____

_____

c)   What happens to sales of domestic cars in the US? Why?

_____

_____

Exercise 10-6.   *US-Japanese Trade Restrictions*

Japan and the US get into arguments over trade on a regular basis, with the US typically accusing Japan of unfair trade practices and threatening to impose trade barriers to the sale of Japanese products (mostly cars and electronics) in the US. Figure 10.1 depicts a trade restriction game between the two countries. This game represents a situation in which the US Congress has threatened to impose new tariffs on Japan to slow the import of Japanese cars into the US. Japan is also considering placing a voluntary export restriction (VER) on its exports. If Japan places a VER on its products, it will voluntarily cut back shipments to the US. If the US places a tariff on Japanese imports, it will make Japanese cars more expensive, also resulting in lower shipments of Japanese cars to the US.

Japan would most prefer to export freely to the US, with no restrictions, either voluntary or imposed. The least-preferred option for the Japanese is to place a voluntary restriction on their exports and also have the US impose additional tariffs. But if some kind of restriction is going to be imposed, the Japanese would rather hold back their own exports (using a VER) than be embarrassed when the US Congress publicly announces that Japan is not trading fairly. Japan would also have more control over a self-imposed VER than over a new complicated trade law written by Congress. So, for Japan, the payoff ordering is as follows:

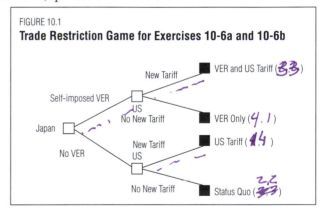

FIGURE 10.1

Trade Restriction Game for Exercises 10-6a and 10-6b

Status quo (SQ) > VER only > US tariff > VER and US tariff

For the US Congress, the least-preferred outcome is to do nothing and allow continued unlimited Japanese exports into the US, because members of Congress and the president are facing domestic pressure to do something about the loss of US jobs to overseas markets. So the status quo is unacceptable and is the worst possible outcome. At the same time, although Congress would like to place some trade restrictions on Japan, it does not want to totally cut off the flow of goods from Japan into the US. So the combination of a VER and additional tariffs is the second-worst outcome. When it comes to a choice of restrictions between a VER and a tariff, assume that Congress would prefer the political statement of imposing a tariff on Japan—this is the best outcome from Congress's point of view. The second-best outcome is for Japan to impose a VER, while Congress holds off on tariffs (this is still much better than having the Japanese continue to export unlimited quantities of goods to the US).

US tariff > VER only > VER and US tariff > SQ

a) Write the preferences for Japan and a punitive Congress in the game in figure 10.1.

b) Solve the game in figure 10.1 by backward induction. Write the complete equilibrium.

Changing the United States' Preferences

Assume now that the US Congress's preferences change.

For Japan: Assume Japanese preferences remain the same as in exercise 10-6.

For the US: Assume that Congress does not care if it totally cuts off trade with Japan and that it wants to punish Japan as much as possible for (perceived) trade violations in the past. For this vengeful Congress, the combination of a VER and additional tariffs is the best possible outcome. The second-best outcome would be a US tariff, while the Japanese do nothing; the third-best outcome would be a Japanese VER with no US tariff; and the worst outcome would again be to do nothing and allow continued unlimited Japanese exports into the US. So:

VER and US tariff > US tariff > VER only > SQ

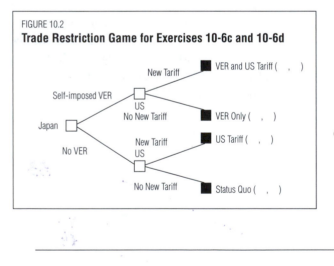

FIGURE 10.2
Trade Restriction Game for Exercises 10-6c and 10-6d

c) Write the preferences for Japan and the vengeful Congress in the game in figure 10.2.

d) Solve the game in figure 10.2 by backward induction. Write the complete equilibrium.

Comparing the Games

e) Compare the games you drew in figures 10.1 and 10.2. How do their equilibria differ? Which actors would choose the same moves, and which would choose different ones?

---

f) You are a Japanese policymaker, and you need to decide whether to adopt a VER. What kinds of evidence might convince you that this US Congress is really of the punitive type and not the vengeful type? Be specific. What information would be convincing and why?

Exercise 10-7. *Protection*

In *Principles*, we began exploring the dynamics between two different sets of producers of widgets, A and B, each producing widget X and widget Y, respectively. All other things being equal, the demand for widget X is inelastic, whereas the demand for widget Y is elastic (or more simply, the demand for widget Y is more elastic than the demand for widget X). The country where these two industries are located is considering opening its border to foreign companies that will bring competition and reduce the domestic prices of widgets X and Y.

a) In this context, which industry will experience a decrease in income?

b) Similarly, which industry will seek protection against international competition?

Exercise 10-8.   *Tariffs*

Following Downs et al.,[1] the utilities for pairs of countries engaged in trade depend on levels of protection. Consider the following utility function for country A, where P^A is the level of protection in country A and P^B is the level of protection in country B:

$$U_A(P^A, P^B) = -(P^B - P_0^B) - (P^A - P_0^A)^2 + \left(\frac{1}{2}\right)(P^B - P_0^B)(P^A - P_0^A) + (P^B - P_0^B)^2.$$

Assume that the utility function for country B is as follows:

$$U_B(P^A, P^B) = -(P^A - P_0^A) - (P^B - P_0^B)^2 + \left(\frac{1}{2}\right)(P^A - P_0^A)(P^B - P_0^B) + (P^A - P_0^A)^2.$$

The levels of protection P are between 0 and 1, that is, zero protection (0% tariffs) and full protection (100% tariffs). Assume that the noncooperative tariffs are $P_0^A = 2/3$, $P_0^B = 3/4$ and cooperative tariffs are $P^A = 1/3$, and $P^B = 1/4$. You can interpret P_0^A and P_0^B as the status quo. Countries can choose either noncooperative tariffs (e.g., $P^A = P_0^A$) or cooperative tariffs.

a) Write down the matrix with payoffs for both players.

b) What is the Nash equilibrium in pure strategies?

---

[1] Downs, George W, David M. Rocke, and Peter N. Barsoom. "Is the Good News about Compliance Good News About Cooperation?" *International Organization* 50, (1996): 379-399.

CHAPTER 11

GLOBALIZATION

International Winners and Losers

Exercise 11-1. *Exchange Rates I*

You are a banker watching exchange rates between the US and Norway. In June 2007, one US dollar was equal to 5.86 Norwegian kroner. You look again in July 2008 and see that one US dollar is now equal to 5.64 kroner.

a) Has the krone gotten stronger or weaker against the dollar?

_____

_____

_____

b) Has the dollar gotten stronger or weaker against the krone?

_____

_____

_____

c) Given your answers to parts a and b of this exercise, will this result in Norway's importing more or fewer goods from the US? Why?

_____

_____

_____

d) Who in the US benefits from the new exchange rate? Why?

_____

_____

_____

e) Who in the US is hurt by the new exchange rate? Why?

_____

_____

_____

Exercise 11-2. *Exchange Rates II*

Now you are a banker watching exchange rates between the US and South Korea. In June 2008, one US dollar was equal to 1,225 South Korean won. You look again in June 2009 and see that one US dollar is now equal to 1,400 won.

a) Has the won gotten stronger or weaker against the dollar?

_____

_____

_____

b) Has the dollar gotten stronger or weaker against the won?

_____

_____

_____

c) Given your answers to parts a and b of this exercise, will the shift in exchange rates result in South Korea's exporting more or fewer goods to the US? Why?

_____

_____

_____

d) Who in the US benefits from the new exchange rate? Why?

_____

_____

_____

e) Who in the US is hurt by the new exchange rate? Why?

_____

_____

_____

Exercise 11-3. *Dollarization*

In 2000, due to hyperinflation and its inability to pay foreign debt, the Ecuadorian government decided to replace its own currency with the US dollar. By the end of that year, the original national currency, the sucre, had disappeared completely from circulation.

Suppose you are an analyst trying to understand the consequences of the dollarization on different aspects of the Ecuadorian economy.

a) How did dollarization affect Ecuadorians' purchasing power? Why?

_____

_____

_____

b) How did dollarization affect the level of foreign investments in Ecuador? Why?

_____

_____

_____

c) How did dollarization affect export industries in Ecuador? Why?

_____

_____

_____

d) How did dollarization affect government spending and the budget deficit? Why?

_____

_____

_____

e) How did dollarization affect government's ability to influence the economy? Why?

_____

_____

_____

Exercise 11-4.   *The Economic Crisis in Greece*

The ongoing deficit crisis plaguing Greece has prompted some observers to suggest that Greece should leave the euro zone and return to its national currency, the drachma. Assume you are an analyst trying to understand the consequences of policy changes that Greece can adopt. Suppose Greece announced that it is leaving the euro zone and returning to the drachma. Next, Greece announced a devaluation of the drachma. Suppose that wages in Greece remained the same.

a) Which sectors would profit from this measure? Why?

_____

_____

_____

b) What would happen to tourism in Greece? Why?

_____

_____

_____

c) What would happen to Greeks' living standards and their purchasing power? Why?

_____

_____

_____

d) What would happen to the prices of imported goods? Why?

_____

_____

_____

e) How would the devaluation affect foreign investment in Greece? Why?

_____

_____

_____

f) Would this measure affect the Greek government's ability to spend money? What would happen to the Greek government's budget deficit and its public debt?

_____

_____

_____

Exercise 11-5. *China's Pegged Currency*

Suppose you are a trade analyst following US-China trade. You know that the Chinese yuan is pegged to the US dollar. You also notice that the Chinese economy has been growing fast, and that the wages of Chinese workers have been increasing.

a) What is the effect of pegging the Chinese yuan to the US dollar on US imports from China? Why?

_____

_____

_____

b) What is the effect of the pegging on foreign investments in China? Why?

_____

_____

_____

c) What are the benefits of a pegged yuan to the US? Who benefits from this policy, and who is hurt by it? Why?

_____

_____

_____

d) Why do some US politicians and observers argue that a pegged yuan is an artificial means of keeping US goods out of China, and increasing the US consumption of Chinese goods?

_____

_____

_____

e) Who would benefit from a floating yuan (in the US, in China, and elsewhere)? Who would be hurt by it (in the US, in China, and elsewhere)?

_____

_____

_____

Exercise 11-6. *Bailing Out Greece*

Greece has been the focus of Europe's debt crisis since 2009. Due to a huge government debt, the Greek government could not meet its obligations. In 2010, Europe's finance ministers together with the International

Monetary Fund agreed to provide a rescue package of more than 100 billion euros as a bailout loan to Greece. The aid was conditional on government spending cuts and restructuring of the debt. A second bailout plan was approved in February 2012, and it is supposed to provide Greece with a financial package through 2014. The expectation is that if the austerity measures are implemented, by 2015 Greece will be able to refinance its debt using private capital markets. In June 2012, following elections and a period of political instability, the new Greek government requested an extension of the bailout deadline from 2015 until 2017. The main European governments, and especially Germany (Greece's biggest creditor), are currently considering the request; their main concern is that the Greek government may not fulfill its promise to cut spending. The following extensive form game captures this negotiation between Greece and Germany regarding extending the bailout deadline in exchange for spending cuts.

Similarly to exercises in chapter 4, assume that there are two players: Germany and Greece. In the beginning of the game, Germany decides whether to extend the bailout deadline or not (*extend / not extend*). If Germany decides not to extend, the game ends. If the bailout deadline is extended, Greece chooses whether to cut spending or not to cut spending (*cut / not cut*). Germany knows that with some probability (R), Greece will not cut spending if the bailout is extended. There are three possible outcomes: (a) no extension of the bailout; (b) Greece receives a bailout extension and cuts spending; and (c) Greece receives bailout and does not cut spending. The players' preferences over these outcomes are as follows:

Germany: (b) > (a) > (c)
Greece 1 (with probability R): (c) > (b) > (a)
Greece II: (b) > (c) > (a)

The game is depicted in figure 11.1. The upper payoff represents the first mover's payoff, and the bottom payoff the second mover's payoff for that particular outcome.

a) If Greece will not cut spending with probability R, what is the probability that Greece will cut spending? Mark this probability on the appropriate branch on figure 11.1.

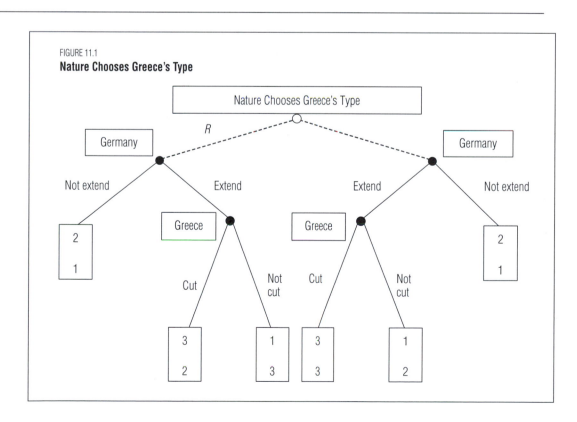

FIGURE 11.1
Nature Chooses Greece's Type

b) Calculate Germany's expected utility for extending the bailout. Show your calculations.

c) What is Germany's utility for not extending the bailout?

_____

d) Under what conditions will Germany extend Greece's bailout? What is the threshold value of R above which Germany will not extend the bailout? Show your calculations.

e) Provide an example of a hypothetical or a real action or statement by a Greek official that would decrease the probability that the bailout is extended. Why would this action have such an effect? Answer in terms of the components of the model in figure 11.1.

_____

_____

_____

f) Which type of Greece (*Greece I* or *Greece II*) can credibly commit to spending cuts, and which type of Greece cannot credibly make such a commitment? Why?

_____

_____

_____

Exercise 11-7. *Factors of Production*

a) According to the US Census Bureau, in 2011 the US imported apparel and household items (textiles) worth almost $37 billion.[1] In the same year, the US exported about $6 billion worth of commodities in this category. Explain this empirical finding in terms of the Hecksher-Ohlin theorem.

_____

_____

_____

b) According to the same source as in part a, in 2011 the US exported over $36 billion worth of plastic materials, and imported about $14 billion worth of commodities in this category. Explain this empirical finding in terms of the Hecksher-Ohlin theorem.

_____

_____

_____

_____

[1] These data are available at http://www.census.gov/foreign-trade/Press-Release/2011pr/final_revisions/#notice_goods (accessed August 24, 2012).

c) According to the Institute of International Education, in the 2009/10 academic year, approximately 128,000 students from China were studying in US universities. In the same academic year, about 14,000 US students were studying in China.[2] Find data about the population size of the US and China in 2009.[3] Next, calculate the percentage of the total US population that studied in China in 2009, and the percentage of the Chinese population that studied in the US in 2009. Explain the difference in terms of the Hecksher-Ohlin theorem. (*Hint:* What is the US exporting when it hosts students from other countries?)

_____

_____

_____

d) Using the data of the Institute of International Education (http://www.iie.org/Research-and-Publications/ Open-Doors/Data), examine the top 10 destinations of US students studying abroad in the 2009/10 academic year. Likewise, examine the top 10 countries of origin of students studying in the US in the 2009/10 academic year. Record the top 10 destinations and the top 10 places of origin in table 11.1.

e) Using the World Bank indicators,[4] obtain the GDP per capita in 2009 in current US dollars for each of the 20 countries in table 11.1 (use the "Economic Policy and External Debt" section). Record the number next to the country's name. Do you see a pattern? How can this finding be explained using the Hecksher-Ohlin theorem?

_____

_____

_____

TABLE 11.1

Top 10 Destinations of US Students Studying Abroad, and Top 10 Countries of Origin of Foreign Students Studying in the US in the 2009/10 Academic Year for Exercise 11-7

Rank	Top 10 Destinations of US Students Studying Abroad	Top 10 Countries of Origin of Foreign Students Studying in the US
1		
2		
3		
4		
5		
6		
7		
8		
9		
10		

---

[2] These data are available at http://www.iie.org/Research-and-Publications/Open-Doors/Data (accessed August 24, 2012).

[3] These data are available on the World Bank website at http://data.worldbank.org/topic (accessed August 23, 2012), under the "Climate Change" section. Look for "Population, total."

[4] These data are available at http://data.worldbank.org/topic (accessed August 23, 2012).

Exercise 11-8. *Mobility and Protection*

Consider two countries: Computerland and Carpetland. Capital is relatively abundant in Computerland, and labor is relatively abundant in Carpetland. There are two products: computers and carpets. The computer industry is capital intensive, and the carpet industry is labor intensive. Computerland is thus more competitive at producing computers and Carpetland at making carpets.

a) Suppose both labor and capital can move freely. If Computerland's government decides to abolish the tariff on imports of carpets, who will profit from this abolishment, and who will be hurt, according to the Stolper-Samuelson theorem? Why?

_____

_____

_____

_____

Now assume that all factors of production are immobile (neither capital nor labor can move across industries or borders). Also assume that there is full employment in the economy (all factors are fully used).

b) Suppose the government of Computerland imposes a new tariff on imports of carpets. Who will the new tariff benefit, and who will it hurt? Why?

_____

_____

_____

_____

c) Computerland's ruling party is interested in attracting the support of the carpet industry before the upcoming election. The party is considering ways to assist the carpet industry in order to appeal to voters who are involved in carpet production. The options are (1) government-funded vouchers for purchasing carpet yarns or (2) tariffs on the import of carpets from Carpetland. If you were advising the ruling party, which type of assistance to the carpet industry would you recommend in order to maximize the industry's support for the party? Why?

_____

_____

_____

_____

Now suppose that labor is mobile, and capital immobile.

d) Do you think labor in Computerland will support imposing tariffs on carpets? Why?

_____

_____

e) Do you think labor in Carpetland will support imposing tariffs on carpets? Why?

_____

_____

f) Do you think capital in Computerland will support imposing tariffs on computers? Why?

_____

_____

g) Do you think capital in Carpetland will support imposing tariffs on computers? Why?

_____

_____

h) Do you think consumers in either Computerland or Carpetland could benefit from a tariff on carpets or on computers? Why?

Extension: Exercise 11-9.   *Invested Interests*

Using your college's or university's library resources, obtain a copy of Jeffry A. Frieden's article, "Invested Interests: The Politics of National Economic Policies in a World of Global Finance," from *International Organization* 45, 4 (Autumn 1991): 525–551. Skim the article and then use that information to help you determine where to read more closely to answer the questions that follow.

a) What are the three Mundell-Fleming conditions? How many can a state have at the same time?

_____

_____

_____

b) What effect of capital mobility causes Frieden to argue that before capital mobility (BCM) and after capital mobility (ACM) political coalition patterns will differ?

_____

_____

c) What are Frieden's three "realistic and analytically useful" reasons for adopting a specific-factors approach?

_____

_____

_____

d) On what two dimensions of exchange rate policy does Frieden base his predictions?

_____

_____

e) In your own words, explain why "producers of nontradable goods and services" are placed where they are in the predictions table on page 545 of the article. (*Hint:* Your response might draw on the concepts in part a of this exercise.)

_____

_____

_____

_____

f) All of Frieden's examples are drawn from the developed world. Consider the interests of domestic groups in a capital-poor country. Do Frieden's predictions for interests in the ACM world seem reasonable in such a situation? Briefly explain why or why not.

_____

_____

_____

_____

CHAPTER 12

FOREIGN AID, POVERTY, AND REVOLUTION

Exercise 12-1. *The Problems of World Politics and the Problems of Foreign Aid*

Principles presented four problems of world politics—coordination, distribution, monitoring, and sanctioning—and asserted that these four problems describe a wide range of behaviors in international relations. This exercise asks you to locate examples (or potential examples) of each of these problems in the politics of foreign aid.

Donors and Recipients

Consider the game played by a potential donor of foreign aid and a potential recipient. Identify an example of each of the problems of world politics in this interaction.

a) Coordination:

Example Answer: Donors and recipients need to coordinate on which projects to fund so that the donor is not giving money for projects the recipient cannot do or does not want.

_____

_____

_____

_____

b) Distribution:

_____

_____

_____

_____

c) Monitoring:

_____

_____

_____

_____

d) Sanctioning:

_____

_____

_____

_____

Between Donors

About 30 different states (and a number of multilateral organizations) give aid. Consider now the game played between donors.

e) Coordination:
    Example Answer: Donors want to coordinate on a plan for funding projects so that they do not fund the same project twice or fund projects that work against one another. These situations waste resources.

    _____

    _____

    _____

    _____

f) Distribution:

    _____

    _____

    _____

    _____

g) Monitoring:

    _____

    _____

    _____

    _____

h) Sanctioning:

    _____

    _____

    _____

    _____

Exercise 12-2. *Aid and Growth*

The determinants of economic growth have been at the center of academic and policy debates for dozens of years. Early theories of growth such as the Solow model argued that economic growth was proportional to investment—if countries manage to invest the necessary resources in capital, they can reach their growth goals. Unfortunately, countries cannot always reach a particular level of investment, leaving them with a financing gap. This financing gap could be filled with economic assistance from other countries.

Suppose that a newly created country such as South Sudan has just finished fighting a civil war. The civil war destroyed all of the country's capital. No factories or machines are available to restart the economy. The new administration recently announced that the economy needs to grow 3 percent in one year.

a) Holding everything else constant, if an annual increase of 4 percent in investment produces an annual increase of 1 percent in total growth, then by how much does investment need to grow in order to reach the 3 percent increase in total growth?

b) If South Sudan can increase investment by only 10 percent a year, what is the financing gap?

c) Discuss issues of coordination, distribution, monitoring, and sanctioning as related to the financing of the gap in South Sudan. Who would give money to South Sudan? Why?

Exercise 12-3.   *The Puzzle of Multilateral Aid*

The argument for foreign aid presented in *Principles* revolves around the goal of obtaining policy concessions in a bilateral (two-state) relationship. A new puzzle arises when considering the 30 percent of official development assistance (ODA) that states distribute through multilateral organizations like the World Bank and the European Union. By definition, that aid is distributed through the organization and is not subject to the decision-making processes or interests of the original state donor.

a) Why might states choose to give aid through multilateral organizations? Explain at least two reasons why states would choose to donate through an organization rather than donate directly to a recipient.

_____

_____

_____

_____

b) Hypothesize about the relationship between multilateral ODA and development outcomes. Should we expect multilateral aid to produce more growth (or poverty alleviation) than bilateral aid, or would it produce the same amount or less growth? Explain the logic behind your hypothesis.

_____

Exercise 12-4.   *Comparing Aid Recipients*

Recipients of ODA vary greatly in their degree of economic and social need, their degree of democracy, and their degree of interest to outside donors. This exercise asks you to collect information about three countries and test them against those three hypotheses of aid receipts. Table 12.1 in *Principles* summarizes the essential points.

The Data

Select one case from each column of countries presented below. Use the coding rules below to complete table 12.1 for your selected cases. As before, most of the data are available from the *CIA World Fact Book* (http://www.cia.gov/library/publications/the-world-factbook) or the Country Pages/Profiles of the British Foreign and Commonwealth Office (http://www.fco.gov.uk) or the US Department of State (http://www.state.gov); additional data on foreign aid are available from the Organisation for Economic Co-operation and Development at http://stats.oecd.org/qwids/. For each piece of data, please indicate the year (i.e., a 2008 estimate of poverty, a 2006 estimate of primary education). You should use the most recent data available.

Libya	Lebanon	Bangladesh
North Korea	Haiti	Turkey
Syria	Belarus	Malawi
Cuba	Tanzania	Nicaragua
Turkmenistan	Pakistan	Palestinian Authority

- Income Classification: Use the World Bank's classifications of upper-middle income, lower-middle income, and low income. These are available from the World Bank at http://www.worldbank.org.
- Poverty T: Percentage of the country's population living at or below the World Bank's poverty threshold of US$2 per day.
- Infant mortality: Death rate among children younger than 5 years of age.

TABLE 12.1

Comparing Aid Recipients

	Case 1: _____	Case 2: _____	Case 3: _____
Independent Variables: Poverty: a) Region			
b) Income Classification			
c) Poverty			
d) Infant Mortality			
e) Literacy			
Democracy: f) Size of W (key member groups)			
g) Size of S (key member groups)			
h) Executive Recruitment			
i) Democracy Summary			
Donor Interests: j) Largest Donor			
k) Strategic Interests			
Dependent Variable: l) Total Foreign Aid			

- Literacy: Percentage of the country's population able to read at an eighth-grade level.
- Size of W: Small, medium, large. Include a brief list of key societal groups (military, single-party members, small business owners, urban labor, etc.) supporting the leader.
- Size of S: Small, medium, large. Include a brief description of what societal groups are members of S.
- Executive Recruitment: Selection or election. See exercise 6-10 for the definitions of these terms.
- Total Foreign Aid: Total aid (grants and loans) received from all sources. These data are available from the US Overseas Loans and Grants Greenbook at http://qesdb.cdie.org/gbk/index.html.
- Major Donor: Identify the actor that provides the largest share (as a percentage of total aid) of the recipient's aid. This may be an international organization such as the World Bank or European Union. These data are available from the US Agency for International Development (USAID) at http://www.usaid.gov/pubs/cbj2002/index.html.
- Strategic Interests: Weak, moderate, strong. Briefly identify any of the donor's strategic or other key interests in the recipient.
- Democracy Summary: Overall assessment of democracy level based on W, S, and Executive Recruitment. Code this variable as in exercise 6-10.

Comparing the Cases

a) Consider your data on need, as indicated in rows b–e. Does higher need appear to be related to higher total aid? (*Hint:* Rank your cases in order of need. Then rank them by total aid. Do the lists match?) Describe the relationship you find: Is it positive or negative? How strong is the relationship?

_____

_____

_____

b) Consider your data on democracy, as indicated in row i. Does more democracy appear to be related to higher total aid? Describe the relationship you find: Is it positive or negative? How strong is the relationship?

_____

_____

_____

c) Consider your data on donor interests, as indicated in row k. Do donor interests appear to be related to higher total aid? Describe the relationship you find: Is it positive or negative? How strong is the relationship?

_____

_____

_____

d) Compare your responses to parts m, n, and o of this exercise. Which of the three competing hypotheses—need, democracy, or interests—does the best job of explaining the pattern of outcomes that you found? Explain your answer.

_____

_____

_____

Exercise 12-5.   _Theories of Assistance_

Principles presents three theories regarding the trouble with economic assistance. Describe each of these theories. Do you agree with them?

_____

_____

_____

Exercise 12-6.   _More on Foreign Aid_

The actions of international organizations can be tightly controlled by their members, such as in the UN Security Council. However, many other organizations implement policies based on simple majority votes. Here, the motions with the most votes are implemented. Countries often lobby other countries to vote for a particular position and exchange economic aid for votes. Japan is particularly effective at providing aid to countries that favor Japan's position in regard to whale hunting.

a) Which countries do you think Japan is more likely to buy off through aid? Give some examples.

_____

_____

_____

Exercise 12-7.   _Democratization and Revolution_

Myanmar is a country in Southeast Asia that is currently experiencing some important political changes. On the one hand, the junta that rules the country has freed Aung San Suu Kyi, the opposition leader, and allowed her to run for parliament. On the other hand, the government has been cracking down on rebels throughout the country.

a) Fill out the following table for Myanmar. As before, most of the data are available from the _CIA World Fact Book_ (http://www.cia.gov/library/publications/the-world-factbook) or the Country Pages/Profiles of the British Foreign and Commonwealth Office (http://www.fco.gov.uk) or the US Department of State (http://www.state.gov); additional data on foreign aid are available from the Organisation for Economic Co-operation and Development at http://stats.oecd.org/qwids/. For each piece of data, please indicate the year (i.e., a 2008 estimate of poverty, a 2006 estimate of primary education). You should use the most recent data available.

TABLE 12.2
Myanmar

Independent Variables	Values
Poverty: a) Region	
b) Income Classification	
c) Poverty	
d) Infant Mortality	
e) Literacy	
Democracy: f) Size of W (key member groups)	
g) Size of S (key member groups)	
h) Executive Recruitment	
i) Democracy Summary	
Donor Interests: j) Largest Donor	
k) Strategic Interests	
Dependent Variable: l) Total Foreign Aid	

b) Use the argument in the "Aid, Revolution, and Democratization" discussion in *Principles* to analyze the current public goods expansion and contraction policies in Myanmar. Make sure to use the argument presented in figures 12.3 and 12.4 in *Principles*.

_____

_____

_____

_____

CHAPTER 13

CAN TERRORISM BE RATIONAL?

Exercise 13-1. *Modeling Terrorism*

Principles discusses a game of terrorism played between any of three types of social groups and either of two types of governments. What we see from the analysis is that although terrorist activity is sometimes carried out by uncompromising individuals who believe in using violence under any circumstances, and who cannot be reasoned with, in other instances it can result from groups of people who would genuinely be willing to talk if the government would let them. However, perceptions are critical to this process and outcome.

Societal Groups

True Believers are committed to violence, even if a government would be willing to talk with them. For them, preferences are Terrorist act > Good-faith negotiations > Being repressed.

Reluctant Terrorists would like to talk, but would rather commit terrorist acts than be repressed by a nasty government. Their preferences are Good-faith negotiations > Terrorist act > Being repressed.

Complacent Opponents would not commit terrorist acts even if they were repressed by a government. They would prefer to talk with a government that might give them what they want, but would accept repression before resorting to violence. Their preferences are Good-faith negotiations > Being repressed > Terrorist act.

Governments

One of the problems with a group that wants to conduct negotiations with a government is that, in some countries, groups do not know what kind of government they are facing. The government might be a type that is willing to listen to problems and negotiate an acceptable political solution for the problems raised by the societal group. But the government might also be one that would use the cover of a negotiation to learn the identities of those who question it and repress them.

Responsive Governments prefer Good-faith negotiations > Repression > Terrorist target.

Nasty Governments prefer Repression > Good-faith negotiations > Terrorist target.

Either type of government least prefers to be subject to terrorist attack, and both prefer repressing a group in society rather than allowing it to conduct terrorist attacks. But they differ in that responsive governments would prefer negotiation to repressing a dissatisfied group in society, whereas a nasty government wants to repress no matter what.

We want to understand what each group in society should do if it wants to be heard. Typically we think that a dissatisfied group should tell its problems to the government in order for the problem to be solved. The alternative is that the group resorts to violence (terrorism) to communicate its message. The difficult part of the decision for a group is that when it goes to the government and offers to talk, it might be met with repression. Depending on the group's type, this may not be an acceptable alternative.

Figures 13.1 to 13.3 show the games played by True Believers, Complacent Opponents, and Reluctant Terrorists.

The game is one of incomplete and imperfect information, and so it starts with a move by nature. The type of incomplete information faced by the group is that the group does not know if it is facing a responsive or a nasty government. We write that with probability p, the government is a responsive type; and with probability $1 - p$, it is nasty.

The choice faced by the group is whether to commit an act of terrorist violence or to request a concession from the government that will satisfy the group politically.

If the group chooses violence, the game ends with a "terrorist act" outcome that leads to no cooperative negotiations and no change in government position.

If the group requests a concession from the government (making its claims public and perhaps asking for a commission to investigate its complaints or to start some kind of negotiation), then the government must decide how to respond. The government can either repress the group or negotiate with it, leading to either a "repression" or "good-faith negotiation" outcome.

The payoffs for each outcome are listed as (group payoff, government payoff).

a) Solve the True Believers game using backward induction in figure 13.1; show your work on the figure. What is the outcome if the government is expected to be responsive? What is the outcome if the government is expected to be nasty? Does the government's type matter? Why or why not?

_____

_____

_____

_____

b) Solve the Complacent Opponents game using backward induction in figure 13.2; show your work on the figure. What is the outcome if the government is expected to be responsive? What is the outcome if the government is expected to be nasty? Does the government's type matter? Why or why not?

_____

_____

_____

_____

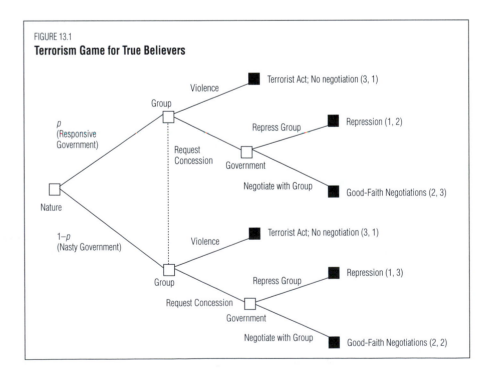

FIGURE 13.1
Terrorism Game for True Believers

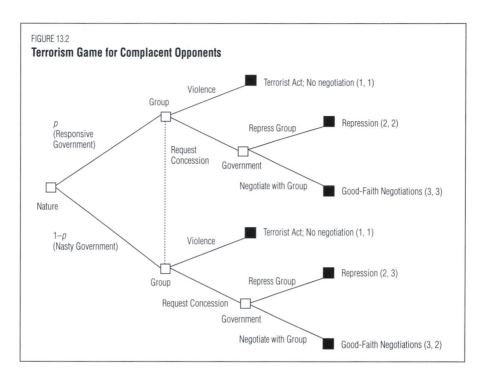

FIGURE 13.2
Terrorism Game for Complacent Opponents

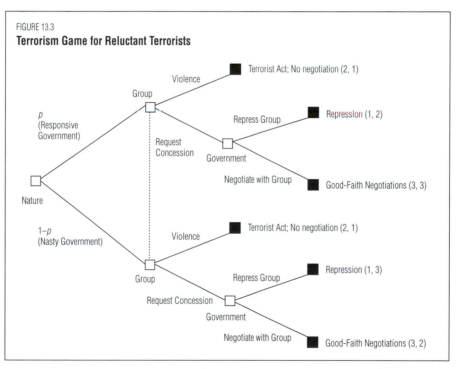

FIGURE 13.3
Terrorism Game for Reluctant Terrorists

c)   Solve the Reluctant Terrorists game using backward induction in figure 13.3; show your work on the figure. What is the outcome if the government is expected to be responsive? What is the outcome if the government is expected to be nasty? Does the government's type matter? Why or why not?

d) The Reluctant Terrorists game shows that violence can occur in a country because of mistaken perceptions and not just because of the presence of fanatics who are set on a violent path. Using insights gained from figure 13.3, explain how violence can result from mistaken perceptions.

_____

_____

_____

_____

_____

Evaluating the Terrorists' Choices

As in our previous games of uncertainty, what is critical in the Reluctant Terrorists game is the potential terrorists' belief about the opponent (here, the government) that they face. We can compute how certain the reluctant terrorists must be to request a concession. To do this, we need to use cardinal payoffs. These payoffs are that $U_{\text{terrorist act}} = 0.4$, that $U_{\text{repression}} = 0$, and $U_{\text{negotiations}} = 1$. The group will request a concession if $EU_{\text{request concession}} > EU_{\text{violence}}$. Consider figure 13.4.

e) Write the expression for $EU_{\text{request concession}}$ in general form (that is, as a formula with no payoffs in it) and then substitute the cardinal utilities. Simplify the expression as much as possible.

f) Write the expression for EU_{violence} in general form (note that this is equal to $U_{\text{terrorist act}}$) and then substitute the cardinal utilities. Simplify the expression as much as possible.

g) Compute the critical value p for which the group will request a concession. What does that value mean? Explain the answer you found.

_____

_____

_____

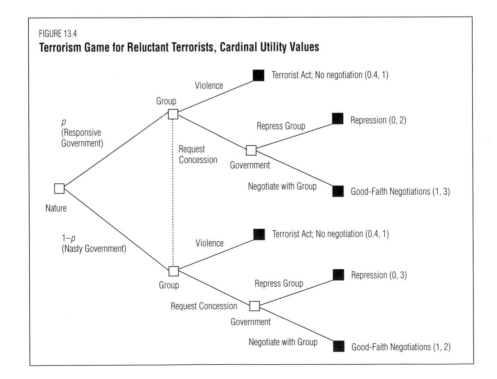

FIGURE 13.4
Terrorism Game for Reluctant Terrorists, Cardinal Utility Values

Exercise 13-2. *Bayes' Rule*

Consider again the game in figure 13.4. Suppose a government official declares that the government will never forgive the terrorists for past violence, and will never acquiesce to their demands.

a) How do you think this statement would affect the group's decision in this game? Would it make the group more or less likely to use violence? Why? Answer using the parameters of the game.

_____

_____

b) Suppose the group's prior belief is that the probability that the government is responsive is 0.5 ($p = 0.5$). Also, assume that there is a 30 percent chance that a responsive government will make such a statement: $p(statement | responsive) = 0.3$. Use the formula for Bayes' rule, and calculate the group's posterior belief that the government is responsive given that it issued such a statement, that is, calculate $p(responsive | statement)$.

_____

_____

_____

_____

_____

c) Compare the posterior belief from part b to your answer in exercise 13-1g. Will the group still request concessions? Why?

_____

_____

_____

_____

_____

Exercise 13-3. *Terrorism and Credible Commitment*

a) Why might a government have difficulty making a credible commitment to terrorists about concessions or negotiations? How does the presence of multiple groups of terrorists help to mitigate this problem?

_____

_____

_____

_____

b) Why might a group of moderates (reluctant terrorists) have difficulty making a credible commitment to the government about restraining any hardliner groups?

_____

_____

_____

c) What incentives do the moderates have to exaggerate their control over the hardliners? What incentives do the moderates have to understate their control over the hardliners?

_____

_____

_____

Considering your answer to part c of this exercise, how might the government try to determine the true level of control that the moderates have? What kinds of things could it do, ask the moderates to do, or look for to help it discover the extent of the moderates' control? Identify two or three of these screening techniques—that is, actions that one party can take to compel another to reveal its private information (here, its type) truthfully.

_____

_____

_____

_____

_____

Why might violence increase following successful negotiations between the government and the moderates?

_____

_____

_____

_____

Exercise 13-4. *A Simultaneous Model of Terrorism*

The game in this exercise depicts an interaction between a government and a group of potential terrorists. In this game, the government may choose one of three moves: do nothing, install passive deterrence measures (like metal detectors at shopping malls and bomb-sniffing dogs on buses), or take active measures (typically, targeting the terrorists with military or special forces attacks). The terrorists can choose from two moves, do nothing or attack. These moves are interdependent because the government's choice of counterterror strategy influences the cost and, likely, success rate (that is to say, the terrorists' expected utility) of violence.

We assume here that the government's move is concealed from the potential terrorists. The potential terrorists do not have complete intelligence on the government's use of its counterterror funds, and so they do not know whether the government has chosen to acquire passive defenses or whether it has prepared an active response. This assumption allows us to model the situation as the simultaneous-move strategic form game shown in table 13.1.

We assume as well that active measures are both more expensive than passive measures and more likely to deter or thwart an attack. Note that the game uses cardinal utilities; some values are negative.

a) Solve this game as we have before. For each of the column player's choices, the row player asks which of her moves makes her best off. For each of the row player's choices, the column player asks which of his moves makes him best off. What, if any, is the equilibrium or equilibria? Show your work, and circle the equilibrium in the table.

TABLE 13.1

Terrorism Game I

		Government		
		Do Nothing	**Passive Measures**	**Active Measures**
Potential Terrorists	**Not Attack**	0, 10	−6, −1	−12, −10
	Attack	10, −10	4, 3	−5, −5

Expanding the Game

The previous game allowed the potential terrorists two moves, do nothing or attack. Let's see now what happens to the game when the terrorists' moves become more complex: they now can choose among doing nothing, staging a small attack, and staging a large attack.

The government spends resources needlessly if it takes active measures against a group that prefers to do nothing. Taking active measures against a small attack is costly but eliminates a future threat. Taking active measures against a large attack is costly, and the attack itself will have some costs.

b) Solve this game as before; please show your work in table 13.2. (*Hint:* We solve this game the same way we did the 2 × 2s and the 2 × 3 above. For each of the column player's choices, the row player asks which of her moves makes her best off. For each of the row player's choices, the column player asks which of his moves makes him best off.) What, if any, is the equilibrium or equilibria?

_____

_____

c) Which player has a dominant strategy? Considering the reasoning behind the other actor's preferences, why does this make sense?

_____

_____

d) Describe the preferred strategy of the player who does not have a dominant strategy. Does this player use all of his or her strategies? If yes, under which conditions (against which opponent move) is each used? If not, which strategy is dominated? (A dominated strategy is one that is never a best response to any move by the opponent.)

_____

_____

_____

e) Compare the games in tables 13.1 and 13.2. What is the effect of adding the third move for the terrorists? In other words, how do our predicted choices and expected outcomes differ across the two games?

_____

_____

_____

TABLE 13.2

Terrorism Game II

		Government		
		Do Nothing	**Passive Measures**	**Active Measures**
Potential Terrorists	**Not Attack**	0, 10	−6, −1	−12, −10
	Small Attack	7, −4	−8, −6	−11, −7
	Large Attack	12, −11	9, −8	−10, −9

When Will the Government Take Active Measures?

f) In part d of this exercise, you should have found that the government will never take active measures. Why? Consider the government's payoffs and justify the preference ordering that makes it prefer passive measures even if faced with a large attack.

_____

_____

_____

_____

g) *Challenge:* Devise and justify a payoff ordering in which the government prefers to take active measures. Show your revised game and its solution, and your justification, on a separate sheet of paper.

h) *Challenge:* Changing the government's payoffs is not the only way to arrive at outcomes in which the government prefers to take active measures. Use the original government payoffs given in table 13.2, but now devise and justify a payoff ordering for the potential terrorists that results in the government's preferring to take active measures. Show your revised game and its solution, and your justification, on a separate sheet of paper.

Exercise 13-5. *Commitment Problem*

Consider the game in figure 13.5. It depicts a strategic interaction between a government and a terrorist group. The government chooses between offering concessions and not offering concessions, and the terrorists choose between attacking and not attacking. There are four potential outcomes: terrorists win, compromise/peace agreement, war, and continuation of the status quo. Below are the players' preference orderings over these outcomes:

Government: Status quo > Peace agreement > War > Terrorists win.
Terrorists: Terrorists win > Peace agreement < War > Status quo.

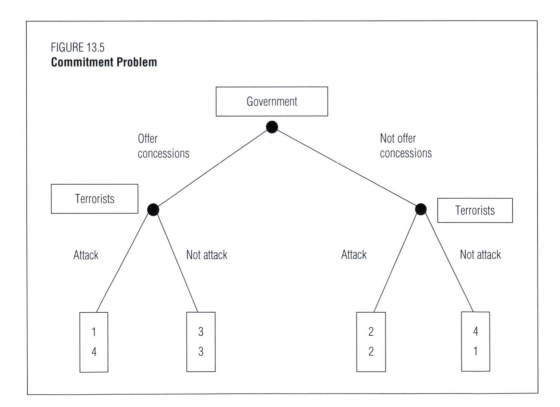

FIGURE 13.5
Commitment Problem

a) Specify the equilibrium strategies of each player.

_____

_____

b) What will be the subgame perfect Nash equilibrium outcome of this game?

_____

_____

c) Is the subgame perfect Nash equilibrium outcome of this game Pareto efficient? If not, then is there another outcome that is Pareto efficient? Why is it not the equilibrium outcome?

_____

_____

d) Is there a commitment problem in this game? If yes, what is this problem, and how does it affect the outcome of the game?

_____

_____

A DEMOCRATIC WORLD ORDER

Peace without Democratization

Exercise 14-1. *Reviewing the Argument*

a) Give two examples of leaders who were removed from office by a foreign power after experiencing military defeat at the hands of that power. Use cases other than Germany or Japan after World War II or Iraq and Afghanistan in the 2000s.

   _____

   _____

b) What type of government did the victor advocate or install in each case in which the defeated state's leader was deposed? Characterize the new governments in terms of their values on *W* and *S*; use our regular coding scheme of small, medium, and large.

   _____

   _____

c) Give two examples of states, other than Iraq and Afghanistan, that experienced a military intervention that led to the creation of a new government or constitution in the occupied/intervened-in state.

   _____

   _____

d) What type of government did the occupier/intervener advocate or install in each case from part c? Characterize the new governments in terms of their values on *W* and *S*; use our regular coding scheme of small, medium, and large.

   _____

   _____

e) Why is installing a democracy (large winning coalition system) in defeated or occupied states not in the interests of the outside power? Identify the type of system the outside or intervening power most prefers and explain why.

   _____

   _____

   _____

   _____

f) Why might a democratic state choose to install a democratic government anyway? How likely is this to happen? Link your answer to the interests of leaders.

   _____

   _____

   _____

Exercise 14-2. *Comparing Postwar Germany and Austria*

At the end of World War II, the four victorious powers occupied Germany and Japan. This fact is widely known. Lesser known, though, is the quadripartite occupation of Austria, which was also considered to be a primary belligerent in the war. Much as they did in Germany, the four Allied powers divided Austria and its capital, Vienna, into occupation zones. In Germany, this process was tense, and the Soviets often refused to cooperate with the other zones even on every-day matters such as the postal service. Ultimately, the three western zones of Germany merged in 1949 and became the (democratic) Federal Republic of Germany. The Soviet zone remained separate and became the German Democratic Republic (Communist East Germany). The hardening of this division is seen by many as one of the first events of the Cold War. Foreign forces remained in both states, and the occupiers continued to exert influence over the foreign policies of both Germanys (though much less so in the West).

In Austria, however, events evolved very differently. Cooperation between the four occupying powers was smooth and effective. By the late 1940s and early 1950s, a coherent national political system existed, and the Austrians began choosing their own leaders to work with the occupying powers. In 1955, the Austrians and the occupiers signed the Austrian State Treaty. The treaty committed Austria to remaining neutral in the emerging Cold War, and Austria declared that it would refrain from joining any alliances. It also created a democratic, mul-tiparty political system and a largely free-market economy. The signing of this treaty ended the occupation and removed all foreign troops from Austria.

The puzzle of the Austrian case is this: Austria and Germany are about as similar as we can possibly hope for on many potential independent variables: educated populations, prior experience with democracy and capitalism, religious and ethnic heritage, geographic region, nature of the nondemocratic interregnum, purpose of the inter-vention/occupation, identity of occupiers (and, subsequently, the size and composition of their winning coalitions and selectorates), acceptance of Marshall Plan aid, etc. We couldn't ask for a closer pair for a natural experiment. We know, though, that we can't explain variables that differ across cases—the outcomes of occupier cooperation and unification—with constants (variables that are the same across cases). If all of these independent variables are constant across the two cases, what explains the variation on outcomes?

a) Propose a hypothesis to explain the variation in occupier cooperation. Indicate your proposed independent variable on the line to the right of the hypothesis, and put an up or down arrow in front of it to indicate whether increasing or decreasing your dependent variable would result in increased occupier cooperation. Then briefly explain the theory behind your hypothesis: Why do you think your proposed independent variable explains the variation in outcomes between the two cases? (*Hint:* You might want to do a bit of research to verify that your variable differs between the two cases.)

↑ occupier cooperation ← _____

_____

_____

_____

_____

b) Propose a hypothesis to explain the variation in post-occupation unification. Indicate your proposed indepen-dent variable on the line to the right of the hypothesis, and put an up or down arrow in front of it to indicate whether increasing or decreasing your dependent variable would result in complete unification after occupa-tion. Then briefly explain the theory behind your hypothesis: Why do you think your proposed independent variable explains the variation in outcomes between the two cases? (*Hint:* Again, you might want to do a bit of research to verify that your variable differs between the two cases.)

↑ post-occupation unification ← _____

_____

_____

_____

_____

c) For one of your hypotheses, briefly identify one type of evidence that would support your argument and one type of evidence that would falsify it. (*Hint:* What types of behaviors—actions, arguments communicated in official memos or documents, issues reported in the newspapers—would you expect to observe if your argument were right, and what would you expect to observe if it were wrong?)

_____

_____

_____

_____

Exercise 14-3.   *Comparing Interventions*

In this exercise, you will explore and compare two interventions. What did the intervener want—what was its motivation for the intervention? Was it successful at achieving its goals? If not, why not? What kind of political system did the intervener (want to) install in the target state?

Choose one case from each column below to complete table 14.1. Be sure to pick two cases from the same era—either Cold War (1946–1990) or post–Cold War (1991–present).

Soviet Union – Afghanistan 1979	US – Grenada 1983
Vietnam – Cambodia 1971	Belgium – Congo 1960
Iraq – Kuwait 1990	US/UN coalition – Kuwait 1991
USSR – Czechoslovakia 1968	South Africa – Lesotho 1998

Code questions about **W**, **S**, Executive Recruitment, and Democracy Summary as in exercise 6-10.

The Data

■ Intervener goals: What were the intervener's public goals or stated motivations for the intervention? You may wish to note if sources indicate a significant divergence between public rhetoric and underlying intentions.

■ Successful intervention: Did the intervention achieve the stated goals? Code this as full, partial, none, or regression. "Regression" in this context refers to a post-intervention status quo that is worse for the intervener than the pre-intervention status quo. This may be an appropriate code, for example, when the attempted intervention was met with force and was repelled, and the target country then attacked the intervener in response.

■ Intervener's preferred regime type: Note here if the intervener made any explicit claims or statements about its preferred post-intervention regime in the target state. If you find no evidence of explicitly stated preferences, code this variable as 0. If explicit claims occurred, code this variable as 1 and note the content of the claims.

■ Post-intervention regime type: Characterize the post-intervention regime in terms of the size of its W and S, both of which are coded as small, medium, or large. Note significant changes, if any, to each from the pre-intervention regime.

TABLE 14.1

Comparing Interventions

	Case 1: _____	Case 2: _____
Era		
Intervener Political Institutions: a) Who is in *S*?		
b) How big is *S*?		
c) Who is in *W*?		
d) How big is *W*?		
Executives: e) Who is the leader?		
f) How did the leader attain office?		
g) Democracy summary		
Target: h) How did the leader attain office?		
i) Democracy summary		
Intervener Motivation: j) Intervener goals		
k) Successful intervention?		
Dependent Variable: l) Hypothesized regime type		
m) Intervener's preferred regime type		
n) Post-intervention regime type		

a) The two lists contain autocratic and democratic interveners, respectively. According to the theory presented in chapter 14, what types of goals should we expect for democratic interveners? What kind of goals should we expect for autocratic interveners?

_____

_____

_____

b) In each case, did the intervening state achieve its goals? If you coded success as yes, briefly describe the evidence to support that coding. If you coded success as no, briefly speculate on why the intervener was unable to achieve its goals.

_____

_____

_____

_____

c) Did the observed post-intervention regime (or intervener regime preferences) match the hypothesized post-intervention regime (or regime preference)? How well does the theory seem to fit the two cases you investigated?

_____

_____

_____

d) This exercise asked you to pick two cases from the same era, either Cold War or post–Cold War. By doing so, we control for that variable—that is to say, hold it constant across cases. As we reviewed in exercise 14-2, we cannot explain a variable (like the different outcomes we observe across the cases) with a constant. Controlling for era allows us to ensure that any difference in outcomes is actually caused by something else—our independent variable of interest, we hope. Let's think about era as a potential causal variable. Does the theory presented in *Principles* give us any reason to believe that the era will matter? Explain your answer: How might era affect our dependent variable, and why might we expect no effect? Do you think we need to control for era here? Why or why not? What other important variables do you think we *should* control in a comparison like this? For one proposed control variable, briefly explain your rationale for why it might influence the outcome (and thus should be controlled).

_____

_____

_____

_____

Exercise 14-4.

According to *Principles*, what are the two exceptions to the theoretical claim that democracies try harder than autocracies in war? Can you think of cases in which autocracies fought as hard as democracies?

_____

_____

_____

Exercise 14-5.

According to *Principles*, it is seldom in the interest of a leader of a democratic intervening state to construct democratic institutions. However, in at least two circumstances, it is in the democratic leader's interest to help another country become democratic. What are these two circumstances? Why are these circumstances difficult to find in practice?

_____

_____

_____

ABOUT THE AUTHORS

Anna Getmansky is a postdoctoral fellow in the Department of Social and Decision Sciences and a visiting fellow in the Center for International Relations and Politics at Carnegie Mellon University. She received her PhD from New York University (NYU). Her research interests include conflict and violence, both inter- and intra-state, and her dissertation considered the effects of domestic politics on government protection from insurgency and terrorism, and on the insurgents' and terrorists' choices of targets. At Carnegie Mellon she teaches courses on terrorism and insurgency as well as international conflict, and she previously taught international relations at NYU.

Alejandro Quiroz Flores is Lecturer (Assistant Professor) in the Department of Government, University of Essex. He obtained his PhD in politics at New York University in 2010, where he was also clinical assistant professor. He specializes in methodology, political economy, and international relations. His work has appeared or is forthcoming in the *British Journal of Political Science*, *International Studies Quarterly*, *Economics and Politics*, *Conflict Management and Peace Science*, and *Foreign Policy Analysis*.

⬤SAGE research**methods**

The essential online tool for researchers from the world's leading methods publisher

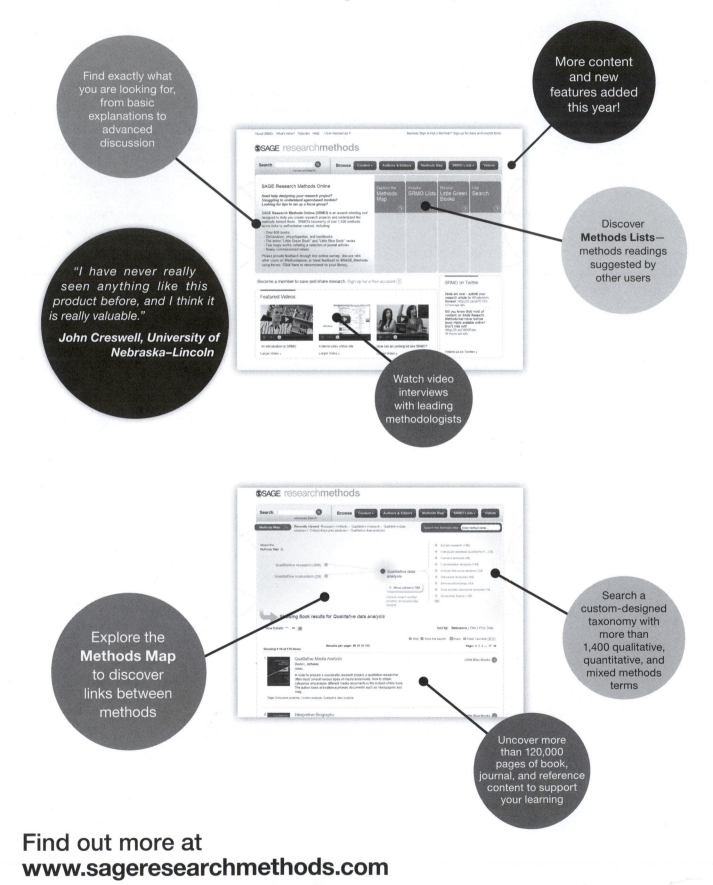

Find exactly what you are looking for, from basic explanations to advanced discussion

More content and new features added this year!

"I have never really seen anything like this product before, and I think it is really valuable."

John Creswell, University of Nebraska–Lincoln

Discover **Methods Lists**— methods readings suggested by other users

Watch video interviews with leading methodologists

Explore the **Methods Map** to discover links between methods

Search a custom-designed taxonomy with more than 1,400 qualitative, quantitative, and mixed methods terms

Uncover more than 120,000 pages of book, journal, and reference content to support your learning

Find out more at
www.sageresearchmethods.com